Bye Bye
Narcissist

Bye Bye Narcissist

Identifying, Understanding, and Leaving the Narcissist in Your Life

Fred L. Holtz, PhD
and Robin Bryman, PhD

To my supportive, patient, and caring wife, Joanne. Thank you for your unconditional acceptance and love. And to my wonderfully precocious son, Aaron, whose kind and generous nature is shining through even before his second year of life.

—*Fred*

To my children, Andie and Zachary. Watching you grow into the kind, compassionate, and empathetic individuals that you are has been the best gift a mother could ask for. And to my husband, Ken. Thank you for always inspiring me to be the best version of myself. I shine brighter with you.

—*Robin*

BYE BYE NARCISSIST

CONTENTS

PART 1
The Narcissist

CHAPTER 3

CHAPTER 4

CHAPTER 5

CHAPTER 6

PART 2

Freeing Yourself from the Narcissist

CHAPTER 7

Bye-Bye, Narcissist!

CHAPTER 8

Hello, It's Me ... 121

CHAPTER 9

Victimized, Not Victim ... 131

CHAPTER 10

All You Need Is Self-Love ... 137

CHAPTER 11

Making the Break ... 167

CHAPTER 12

Building New Relationships ... 175

CHAPTER 13

On the Move ... 193

CHAPTER 14

Share the Joy ... 201

CHAPTER 15

A Special Message for Therapists (and Clients) ... 205

FOREWORD

It is nearly impossible to say anything new about the topic of narcissistic abuse these days. Or so I thought before I came across this book. It is a dialogue between two professional clinical psychologists, Dr. Fred Holtz and Dr. Robin Bryman, who fell prey to narcissists. They don't always see eye to eye and this fertile tension renders this collaboration a unique offering in the field.

Narcissistic abuse, unlike any other form of abuse, is about negating the totality of the victim, rendering them mere extensions, functions, or instruments. It is the ultimate form of objectification and dehumanization. But, thirty years ago, people lacked the forum, framework, and language to talk constructively about their experiences of narcissism.

In the early 1990s, few people had heard of narcissism. So, in 1995 I wrote *Malignant Self-love: Narcissism Revisited* and, two years later, I created a website and uploaded to the Internet a free electronic edition of that book, which is still available at Narcissistic-Abuse.com. That was the first website ever devoted to narcissism. It generated an outpouring of anguish and relief from both narcissists and victims of abuse, who now could put a label to their misery and suffering. Thus, we followed up with the first print edition of the book in 1999, currently in its tenth edition.

At the time, with the exception of a handful of scholars, no one had even heard of pathological narcissism. I had to come up with a whole new vocabulary to describe the pernicious disorder and its insidious effects. I coined phrases such as somatic and cerebral narcissist, narcissistic abuse, no contact, devalued and discarded, cold empathy, hoovering, flying monkeys, and dozens of others. Sometimes, I had to imbue moribund phrases from the 1930s and 1970s with new meaning: narcissistic supply, gaslighting, and false self are three examples of many.

Now in 2023, narcissism is a cultural meme, a buzzword, and a leading topic of study in academe. Yet, it is precisely this popularity that threatens to obscure the true nature of Narcissistic Personality Disorder—a threat Dr. Holtz and Dr. Bryman effectively address in personal and practical terms.

This book is a breath of fresh air and a new promise of rigorousness and clarity. Replete with useful checklists, case studies, and personal narratives, this book is a cornucopia. Two delightful chapters are dedicated to narcissism in literature and to *Alice's Adventures in Wonderland* and *The Wonderful Wizard of Oz*, as parables of narcissism. The entire cycle—from love bombing to hoovering and the aftermath—is meticulously analyzed in an accessible, helpful fashion.

I found myself riveted by its narrative style and even learned a thing or two! I can't recommend *Bye Bye Narcissist* enough.

SAM VAKNIN

Author of *Malignant Self-love: Narcissism Revisited*

Why We Wrote This Book

Almost everyone has had a bad relationship. They hurt. They can be emotionally devastating. But they are not the same as a narcissistic relationship, which leaves you feeling mentally twisted, confused, self-doubting, destroyed, and shocked. The aftereffects and trauma of a narcissistic relationship are psychologically different. They are uniquely damaging to the heart, mind, and spirit. If you've been there, you understand that you are (or were) in the presence of pathology, deep emotional sickness, purposeful destruction. Evil.

One purpose of this book is to provide you the comfort of knowing that you are not alone. Your feelings and thoughts are perfectly normal, given your exposure to a narcissist. So we will have lots of real-life examples from people who have been there. You will need to understand what a narcissist is, what tactics they use, and that they will not "get better." You will need to be aware of the devastating effects that are always associated with being in a pathological relationship. And, finally, in order to move on to a healthier, sane life, you will have to work on yourself, care for yourself, and recover from the ordeal of narcissism.

This book will be the first resource you pick up when you think that nobody will understand what you are going through. We understand because we have been there. There is hope and a better life at the end of the tunnel. You can and will survive, *thrive*, and be a better, stronger, and more insightful person for having experienced this horrible ordeal. And even though right now it seems as if everyone is a narcissist, you will discover that there are actually some great, positive people out there.

The book grows out of our own experiences. Robin and I share our stories as an illustration of the challenges and dangers of being in a relationship with a narcissist. We wrote this book to help you realize that you are not alone, to give you useful information to identify narcissistic abuse, and to guide you in safely leaving an abusive relationship.

DR. FRED

I was just like anyone else getting stuck in a pathological relationship with a narcissist. It was exciting at first: lots of talk about being "soulmates," super-romantic expressions, deep discussions. She was fascinating, unique, had a compelling backstory, and seemed to cherish the same values I did. We appeared to be in similar situations in life, even though we were from different cultures. I believed this was a match with lots of potential.

One of her first emails was a list of provocative, complicated questions about beliefs, experiences, dreams, and opinions. I was instantly intrigued, and I responded with a lot of thought and enthusiasm. Since I have a background in creative writing and philosophy, I enjoy thought-provoking questions. In retrospect, I can see how this first approach "hooked" me.

After a short period of normalcy, something felt extremely wrong. I was surrounded by red flags but somehow was blind to them. After I described a certain incident to my best friend, he said he couldn't understand why I would tolerate such strange behavior. I felt trapped, stuck, unable to act. The relationship felt like an addiction.

My closest friends and colleagues know me as an optimistic, high-energy, positive person. But I soon found myself depressed, lost, lonely, and isolated from my friends and family. The best and simplest description of how I felt was "not myself." I was neglecting my business. I was usually a frenzy of fresh ideas, but my creativity was sapped. Nonsensical arguments and weird demands were draining all my energy.

Regardless of the multitude of warning signs, I was hooked. We were engaged, and I married her. Of course, she did not like the engagement ring, so we exchanged it for another. She changed the wedding date three times so she could find a calendar day that had the right "spiritual energy." The manipulations continued, and the abuse got worse.

I went through torturous mind games, wondering, "Is it me?" Since I had been previously married and divorced, this was a legitimate concern. I looked at literature on codependency, but it did not seem to fit my situation. I reviewed my family background. Though it was certainly not perfect, I grew up with two parents who cared deeply about their family, easily and openly expressed affection both between themselves and with their children, and struggled financially at times but certainly provided all the necessities and some luxuries. My siblings and I were listened to, nurtured, and never physically disciplined or emotionally abused. Loving grandparents were always part of the home experience. My middle-class, mostly typical, suburban Long Island upbringing could not be blamed for my strange attachment to this little narcissist. I was losing sleep, perpetually searching my soul, trying to figure out what was happening. What would keep me in a relationship like this one? Why was I stuck? I saw the red flags. They were obvious. Why hadn't I paid attention and left long ago? What's going on here? And, ultimately—what is wrong with me?

I had always been a big fan of Dr. John Gottman, the leading expert on pragmatic ways to find and preserve loving relationships. Informed by his work, I attempted to have calm, nonaccusatory, "I" statement–filled discussions with my narcissistic wife, always thinking, "I can fix this!" I tried every known approach recommended by the world's best relationship experts (including what I'd learned from my own parents). I found myself apologizing constantly to preserve the peace, even though for the life of me I never could figure out what I had done wrong. I agreed to marital therapy, and we found a seasoned, licensed professional. After two sessions of throwing me under the proverbial bus, the narcissist insisted that I continue alone. After one individual session, the psychologist looked at me in silence for a moment, then confidently said, "Run!"

But I didn't run. I tried everything under the sun to make the marriage work. The narcissist had already reminded me a million times that everything was my fault and that I had previous "failed marriages." She constantly asked, "Who would ever want someone like you?" Along with daily cursing, she made weird demands, gave me frequent silent treatment, idolized her previous relationships, engaged in embarrassing public tantrums and pathological jealousy, and interfered inappropriately with my private practice. Her tactics also included a very persistent campaign, ultimately successful, to alienate my own relatives from me.

Finally, this was rock bottom. It was difficult for me to admit that I was being abused. It was even tougher, as a man, to reveal that I was being abused by a woman. I know that sounds ridiculous in retrospect, but the notion was very salient at the time. Like others who are finally coming to their senses and waking up to the reality of being emotionally abused, I needed assistance. Dr. Tara Palmatier, founder and owner of the Shrink4Men franchise, was immensely helpful in this regard. Also, just like almost everyone I have spoken to in similar situations, I sat down and typed the word *narcissist* in my Google search bar. Even though I am a licensed psychologist and have been for over thirty years and am probably considered to be an "expert" on personality disorders and psychopathology, I resorted to a Google search for validation.

Regardless of training, intelligence, or professional degrees, I could not have escaped without guidance and support. And I'm going to be blunt: neither can you. Almost every member of the weekly support group that I facilitate has an advanced degree (law, medicine, financial) or would otherwise be considered a "professional." It doesn't matter. All were suckered in and abused by their little narcissists. It is crucial to keep in mind that your narcissist is also a "professional" at what they do. They have done their research, practiced and honed their skills, and carefully selected their target. They will not change. You cannot beat them at their own game because, luckily, you are not a psychopath. You cannot beat the narcissist, but you *can* escape and get your life back.

DR. ROBIN

 Imagine thinking clearly, being able to make thoughtful decisions, feeling calm, confident, and happy. Being in a relationship with a narcissist destroys all those peaceful feelings. You feel quite the opposite, as though you are walking around in a fog. You also feel like you've been hit by a truck. You're a shell of who you once were. Without being aware of it, you've allowed the narcissist to take away people you've loved, your productivity, your bright energy, and your self-esteem.

That was me. I allowed that to happen. Yes, I survived; since healing, I've thrived. I've never been more content or more productive in my life. However, I continue on my healing journey to this day by helping others. I truly understand the healing process because I've been trauma-bonded to a covert malignant narcissist. For those who are in this stage of narcissistic abuse, please know that if you do the work in healing your codependency, you will get better. The fog will eventually lift, and you will love yourself again. Welcome to this incredibly painful but transformative journey through the recovery process. It is much more rewarding than you can ever possibly believe.

The narcissist entered my life when I was vulnerable. Life tends to have ups and downs, and I would say that it was a down time for me. Looking back, I realize how much of a spiritual journey it's been for me and how the narcissist, and narcissists in general, have a sixth sense about whom they can prey on and target. I remember when he said hello to me for the first time. I had a visceral, physical reaction. Almost as if I'd been struck by lightning. One might say it was a love-at-first-sight feeling. Later I realized, as a codependent person, that my programming was off. I thought it was butterflies in my stomach, but what it turned out to be was an intuition in my gut that I ignored. It felt like a mix of excitement and anxiety. That feeling remained potent for the years that I was with the narcissist.

Prior to meeting the narcissist, I was a high-achieving rule follower who was perhaps too trusting and too quick to see the best in people. Looking back, I realize that I personally subscribed to the belief that others thought the same way I did. I realized that I learned this rigid style of thinking in childhood. My eighty-seven-year-old parents to this day are still in love and devoted to each other and to their children, grandchildren, and great-grandchildren. They are products of their own upbringing and, as a result, had a traditional marriage and raised three high-achieving children with good values. As lifelong generous givers and people pleasers, my parents are wonderful and caring people, albeit codependent, naïve about whom they trust, and not very grounded in their own personal identities.

My relationship with the narcissist left many emotional scars. Over time, my scars have healed as I have developed knowledge about who the narcissist was and who I was, and who I eventually became as a result of the relationship. When I discovered what was happening after being caught up in his covert cycle of emotional abuse—love bombing, devaluation, discarding, hoovering—I felt a huge surge of energy come back to me. I felt as if that fog had finally lifted.

By that point, I had already mentally left the narcissist and begun healing my codependency issues. Because of my psychological background, I started frantically researching: reaching out to colleagues who specialized in personality disorders and even traveling to speak to experts in the field. When I was able to physically leave the narcissist behind, I never *ever* looked back. I promised myself that once I began to thrive, I would help others. As a child psychologist, my goal is to help children and adolescents understand and be able to identify patterns of abuse that are endemic to being in a relationship with a narcissist. Social media and texting are, unfortunately, breeding grounds for this.

One more thing: when I come across someone who flippantly throws the term "narcissist" around, I smile to myself and am thankful to be on this beautiful spiritual journey.

A FINAL NOTE

While we share most fundamental perspectives on narcissism, our views sometimes differ. Robin and I are each embracing our own unique journey. As in any collaboration, we don't see eye to eye on everything. We believe the reader will benefit from these differences in perspective and gain a broader sense of narcissistic abuse.

PART 1

The Narcissist

1

The "Narcissist and You" Checklist

Chances are you already know that you're dealing with a narcissist, or at least suspect that something is very, very wrong. If you need concrete validation, this chapter is for you. We figured that if you are reading this book, you might want to cut right to the chase.

THE CHECKLIST

We have compiled a checklist to help you better understand your relationship, your significant other, and yourself. Check which of these qualities and circumstances apply to you or the probable narcissist, then have a look at our scoring guidelines following each list. Keep in mind that some of these circumstances are more critical than others, and endorsing even one item can mean that it's time to think about leaving.

• • •

ABOUT THEM

My Partner, Spouse, Sibling, Child, Boss, or Coworker

Traits	Yes	No
Does not seem to show empathy or compassion toward other people, including me		
Seems to lie, distort the truth, withhold information, or change his or her story		
Is jealous of other people's accomplishments and successes		
Seems often manipulative or forces his or her opinions on others		
Attempts to make things appear to be others' fault rather than taking responsibility		

Traits	Yes	No
Is controlling of most situations		
Acts in an abusive, demeaning, neglectful, or dismissive way		
Does not take responsibility for his or her own actions and bad behavior		
Is emotionally unavailable and continually ignores or disregards my needs		
Uses the silent treatment often or withdraws when it would be more appropriate to communicate		
Comes on strong, extremely romantic, or idealistic at the beginning of the relationship		
Belittles my opinions		
Always plays the victim		
Tries to embarrass or humiliate me, often in public		
Emphasizes my past mistakes, weaknesses, and failures to avoid a focus on his or her present wrongdoings		
Doesn't ever seem to change, at least not permanently		
Doesn't ever apologize		
Becomes angry when confronted with his or her own actions		
Establishes double standards for acceptable behaviors		
Provokes me, and then blames me for my reactions		
Twists my words or "puts words in my mouth" in arguments		
Points out my imperfections, past and present		
Remembers minor things that happened years ago, or brings up issues that have been settled		
Knows exactly how to push my buttons		
Has a history of broken promises about improving his or her attitude or behaviors		
Turns my friends and family against me		

Traits	Yes	No
Corrects me constantly		
Tries to control my spending		
Accuses me of things I didn't do and couldn't even conceive of doing		
Exaggerates his or her own accomplishments and achievements		
Has an attitude of entitlement and superiority		
Compares me to other people		
Is inconsistent or secretive concerning details about his or her past		
Withholds attention and affection as manipulation or punishment		
Forces his or her own sexual desires and romantic ideas while ridiculing my desires and preferences		
Has a sense of entitlement and requires constant, excessive admiration		
Expects to be recognized as superior even without achievements that warrant it		
Exaggerates achievements and talents		
Believes he or she is uniquely superior and can associate only with equally special people		
Monopolizes conversations and belittles or looks down on people he or she perceives as inferior		
Fails to recognize the needs and feelings of others		
Displays unwarranted jealousy regarding friends, coworkers, or family		
Has difficulty regulating emotions and behavior		
Seems to be collecting information on my weaknesses and vulnerabilities, instead of genuinely caring about me		

Scoring

Checking "yes" on any of the above items is cause for concern. They are all signs of a narcissistic, toxic person. If you checked only one to five items, there is still some cause for concern. These are signs of a relationship in trouble and elements of a personality disorder. If you checked six to ten items, there is a very good chance that you are in the presence of a narcissist. It would be rare for a normal person to display that many troubling behaviors. More than ten items: You need to start planning your escape now. You are in danger.

ABOUT YOU

While in a Relationship with a Suspected Narcissist

Traits	Yes	No
I feel compelled to apologize just to keep the peace, even though I did nothing wrong		
I have become isolated from my friends and family		
I just feel that I am not myself anymore		
I am experiencing anger, frustration, and hopelessness that I have never experienced before		
I have significantly lowered my expectations of this relationship		
I have found myself looking up "narcissist" online		
I always seem to fall short of my partner's (boss's, parent's) expectations		
I experience guilt about my situation		
I feel like I am walking on eggshells most of the time		
I find that I often have to explain my feelings, even though they should be obvious		
I am left feeling crazy and confused after arguments		
I have a feeling something is wrong, but it's difficult to pinpoint exactly what it is		
I feel as if my feelings are not acknowledged		
It's difficult to explain to others the things that go on in my life		
I sound crazy when I try to describe the things that happen in this relationship		
I feel that nothing I do is right in this relationship		
I have been called a narcissist by my partner		
I am not sleeping as well as I used to		
I am not as productive as usual		

Traits	Yes	No
I am anxious and depressed much more than usual		
I feel lost, stuck, overwhelmed, or numb		
I am coping with my feelings in unhealthy ways (drinking, smoking, spending too much, eating differently)		
I have become short-tempered, intolerant, and snappy with those I am close to		
I often have thoughts of leaving, divorcing, quitting (my job), or moving away		

Scoring

It is not normal to be experiencing any of these feelings persistently in a healthy relationship. If you checked one to five items, there is cause for concern, especially if you feel this way most of the time. These are the emotional effects of being in a psychopathic relationship. Take this as a serious call to action. If you checked six to ten or more items, you are already experiencing symptoms of PTSD or other disorders as a result of exposure to a narcissist. You are in a toxic relationship. These symptoms are extremely serious, and you need to take action immediately. If you scored high on both checklists, the matter is even more urgent. Please use this book as a reference for information about narcissism, coping, and recovering from emotionally abusive relationships. Do not hesitate to seek professional help from a mental health or medical professional immediately if you are having serious negative thoughts or ideas.

WHY DID THE NARCISSIST CHOOSE ME?

You are not necessarily "codependent." You are not defective. You are not necessarily an "empath." You have been victimized, but you can stop being a victim right now. The narcissist definitely did choose you. He or she stalked, researched, and targeted you. The narcissist sensed, consciously and subconsciously, that you would be an excellent "supply" (a steady source of attention, admiration, and loyalty) and already had a specific plan to manipulate, abuse, and take advantage of you. The narcissist then continued to gather a catalog of your vulnerabilities and deepest insecurities for later exploitation.

QUESTIONS AND ANSWERS

Reading about narcissists can take you only so far. The question is, What can you do about this person—today? Later in the book, we will present a multistep process for reclaiming your life. At the end of most chapters, the authors will address common issues that have been brought up during seminars and individual therapy sessions and will answer questions based on their own experiences of recovering from narcissistic abuse.

QUESTION: What were a few of the red flags that you first noticed about the narcissist you were with?

DR. FRED

The very first red flag was raised, in my case, when I was describing a specific incident to my best friend. Some of the details are a bit fuzzy at the moment, but it had something to do with my ex having a strange attitude toward my adult daughter. This was early in the relationship, before the two had ever met. My ex made an insulting and judgmental remark. In hindsight, I can see that she was probably disturbed because I had shown that there were, in fact, other cherished people in my life. My best friend said, "That's a really weird thing for her to say. I don't know how you put up with that." Considering that this person had been my closest pal for over forty years and that he knew me inside and out, his comment had a lot of significance. Of course, it remained unheeded.

Another red flag was my ex's very inconsistent telling of her background story. Her descriptions of her family and relationship history were very vague. There were intriguing events with colorful characters involved, but the story of her life, at least as she relayed it, never made sense as a whole. Many of the situations she described seemed unlikely, at best. Sometimes, it seemed, she subtly changed certain facts about past relationships. This was another early red flag. And yet . . .

She had an absolute, full-time obsession with *my* past, endlessly asking millions of questions, "researching," and apparently digging around for any scrap of something negative to focus on. At one point, she even contacted an ex-girlfriend. This was the third red flag (of many). As is often posted in the excellent Shrink4Men Instagram account, this was not normal!

Another profound sign was the ridiculous level of importance that she placed on her work and achievements, while regarding my accomplishments as "childish bragging" or "showing off." Everyone should be proud of what they achieve, but regarding everything you do as the most important endeavor in the world gets tiresome. A related red flag was a pathological jealousy of anything that was enjoyable to me—hobbies, reading, music—because these things took my attention and thus took attention away from her.

DR. ROBIN

I noticed several red flags that eventually became a theme throughout the relationship. One was his overwhelming hatred toward others. He would come home from work or from a social situation and would say awful things about everyone in his life. The energy from him was overwhelmingly negative and draining. Another red flag was how much he gossiped about, smeared, and triangulated others. Over time, his stories didn't make sense, and friends that were close to me grew concerned and confided in me. In addition, his sense of humor had a lot to be desired, as it was exclusively about making fun of others.

2

What Is a Narcissist?

YOU ARE NOT ALONE

Are you in a relationship in which you feel isolated, trapped, confused, and perpetually sad? Have you tried to leave the relationship but feel powerless or unable to do so? Do you feel at a loss to explain what went wrong? Do you keep trying regardless of loneliness, loss of identity, and constant criticism? Are these feelings familiar?

Your relationship began like a fairy tale. Your significant other noticed you, then sent you the most beautiful texts, showering you with attention and, soon, love. You're special, you were told, and you really were made to feel that way. You felt as if you were part of a magnificent, irresistible future—it was that wonderful! Your life, your world, had changed! You were with someone who planned to take the world by storm, who spelled out a wonderful future for the two of you, and whose every word seemed possible.

Soon, your other relationships paled compared to this one. Your new love filled your world and seemed only too happy to do so. Who wouldn't want such beautiful love lavished on them?

But one day, everything changed. You had no idea what you'd said or done, but your new love turned on you, stinging you with insults and cruelty that were hard to fathom. Your partner called into question your connection to reality. You were told that things you knew to be true, were sure to be true—memories you held dear and shared—were not true and never had been. How could that be? Confusion reigned.

And it got worse. This person had once told you that you were everything to them, and now you were nothing. The insults were so painful, you decided to end the relationship, whereupon you were told you would never survive on your own. Your once-exalted love was now unwanted. Your attempts to leave were exhausting. How could someone who adored you turn on you like this?

And then, insanity! This person very, very convincingly told lies about you to your friends and family—lies that painted you as a villain in this relationship. These lies accused *you* of doing things that your former lover did. You grew desperate to get away but found it impossible to do so. You began to question yourself as the stress of this horror of a relationship became intolerable. You no longer recognized your lover, yourself, or your world. All that was yours was suddenly at risk: your home, wealth, friends, country, children, career, energy, creativity, religion, spirituality. Your treasured universe, which had taken a lifetime to build, was falling apart.

If these feelings seem familiar, you may be in a relationship with a narcissist. The above scenario describes a narcissistic relationship. Narcissists attract a partner by "love bombing," or showering attention and lavishing love on the target. In most cases, narcissists target their victims and screen them for specific traits. Once the target is ensnared, the narcissist weaves a web of deception, promises, and lies. Attempts to question or leave are met with venomous attacks, manipulation of reality, and, inevitably, nasty threats.

The scenario below focuses on a different relationship, yet many of the same components of a narcissistic relationship are there.

Emotionally healthy people are unique, but narcissists are all very much alike, despite differences in age, race, gender, nationality, and religion. The arsenal the narcissist employs to attract, trap, and poison his or her victim is nearly always the same.

Your mother, father, sibling, or adult child dominates and at the same time is absent from your life. This family member demands constant attention and stroking, twists the truth, and twists your words. Where once your relationship had seemed loving, it is now toxic. You give and give and give more, and they take and take and accuse you of all sorts of evils. You are told that everyone will learn the truth about you if you don't do what you're told. You endure hurtful, demeaning, and shaming untruths about yourself, and this person assures you that everyone else will hear these things. And you believe the falsehoods, because they are twisted, distorted versions of the truth that sound entirely plausible.

The usual boundary-setting strategies are not effective with the narcissist. Calling the narcissist a narcissist seems only to strengthen the neural grip holding the two of you together. Like a misbehaving child, the narcissist welcomes attention, whether positive or negative. Attempting to explain the narcissist's twisted and manipulative behavior to others can lead to *you* sounding like the crazy one. It is extremely difficult to capture in words the illogical circumstances and convoluted tactics of the narcissist.

Narcissism can manifest itself in just about any relationship, wreaking havoc on love and family and poisoning the home or work atmosphere. A narcissistic coworker, for example, can attempt to create the appearance that you are ineffective, lazy, behaving maliciously toward other employees, or insubordinate in some way.

A narcissistic employer is in an even better position to rig the work environment against you.

Ever since your second month at your job, your supervisor has distorted your role when presenting your department's achievements to

C-level executives. At first, you were welcomed with open arms, your attributes recognized and lauded and your early achievements earning plaudits. But ever since you casually mentioned your role in a company success and disagreed with your supervisor at a company meeting, your supervisor has changed, insisting on taking credit for every success and spreading lies and innuendos about you, leading to constant conflict and a toxic work environment. Now you are shunned by your coworkers and expected to do more, while getting no credit for your work.

Narcissism is commonly misunderstood as simple self-centeredness or is described as being similar to egotism. "It's always about them," we might think about someone, labeling them a narcissist. While it *is* always about the narcissist, there is much more to narcissism than self-centeredness.

EXAMPLES OF NARCISSISTIC MANIPULATION

Here are some more specific examples, this time from people who have been abused by narcissists. These may resonate with you and be difficult to read:

SHERYL'S STORY

We were at a costume party where there was a DJ and a dance floor with a loud sound system. He forced me to ask the DJ to pause the music, and he had me publicly apologize for some perceived transgression, as well as publicly admit that I was a liar. To this day I cannot believe that I actually listened to him and did it! It was a horrific embarrassment. And, of course, there never was any real "transgression" to begin with! I just wanted the argument to stop. In the end, of course, I hadn't apologized "correctly," so it didn't count. Later that evening he demanded that I get down on my knees and beg for forgiveness. I'm so ashamed to say this, but I did that too. Anything to stop the emotional torture.

Desiring an apology after a disagreement is not abnormal. The scenario above, however, is absolutely not normal. The depersonalizing, control, paranoid accusations, and demeaning demands are absurd. These are the telltale signs of a narcissist in a pathological relationship.

BOB'S STORY

My wife had been giving me the silent treatment all day. While we were stopped at a red light on a busy highway, she told me to admit that all the problems in our relationship were my fault and that I was a bad person. I responded, "Who would ever say something like that?" This infuriated her and she followed up with, "If you don't admit this right now, I am getting out of this car!" I refused, and she got out of the car in the middle of a large, busy intersection, causing a tremendous scene. I felt I couldn't just let her walk around an unfamiliar area of the city alone, so I followed her around to make sure she was safe while she cursed out loud and called me every name in the book until she finally agreed to get in the car and come home. Later, she blamed me for "making her" leave the car and be in a dangerous place. I still have no idea what prompted this outburst (one of many), and it was never really settled. The antics were astounding.

If you've read this far, you can probably think of a few examples from your own relationship just like these. They seem crazy because they are. These are not "normal" interactions. They aren't even normal arguments. They are products of a pathological relationship. It often seems that these narcissists all get the same memo or are all reading from the same playbook. The examples have an eerie similarity.

CATHY'S STORY

One night, my boyfriend had to work late. I wanted to surprise him with a nicely prepared dinner, so I looked up a recipe for his favorite meal and timed it so it would be ready just when he got home. He barely greeted me when he arrived. Once the table was set, he immediately seemed unhappy. We got into an argument because, he told me, I hadn't prepared the carrots "properly." I had sliced them into little round medallions instead of long strips. I responded by saying, "No problem. Next time I'll do it the way you like." It seems ridiculous to even describe, but he became infuriated over this. I attempted to ask him if there was something else that was bothering him besides the carrots. He threw his plate in the sink, stormed out, and wound up locking himself in the guest bedroom, refusing to discuss the issue. It's my nature to resolve things calmly and quickly, but my attempts were met with the silent treatment, even into the next day. He never ate the dinner. Whatever issue sparked this conflict was never discussed or settled.

The insults, the attempts at control, the juvenile tactics. Who would ever put up with these antics? But we do. We tolerate them and even try to abide by their pathological agendas.

FLORENCE'S STORY

If I inadvertently mentioned a person with the same first name as one of my ex-boyfriends, the narcissist reacted as if I was cheating on him. Any discussions about previous relationships, except *his*, of course, were strictly forbidden. One time I received a spam call from some lending organization that came up on my iPhone as a male name. He went ballistic because he didn't like the way I "reacted" when I hung up. He claimed I was happy to see the name on my phone. I told him I didn't think that way; I wasn't even capable of thinking that way and it wasn't anywhere in my thoughts. This led to an evening of arguing, and I still have no idea what he was talking about.

JULIE-ANNE'S STORY

He told me I'd be living in the street without him. He said that very soon after we had moved out of state. I didn't believe him, but I did understand how hard it would be to live thousands of miles from my family without a means of support. There was some truth to his threats.

TERESA'S STORY

I can't do much of anything because of my money situation. I had quit a pretty good job because of him. He had promised he would support me forever and treat me like a queen. Now, I pray to be able to get away. We're both handicapped. In my earlier marriage I was young, employed, and had a more hopeful attitude. Now, not so much. I gave up on happiness.

DORIS'S STORY

He told me I would never get by without him. And you know what? It wasn't easy, in part because he had me convinced this was true. My own mind was part of the problem because I believed him! I had trouble functioning on my own for years. I was scared. I tried to communicate with my family, but he had poisoned them—some of them anyway. I'm doing better now, but it took work. A lot of it!

DAVID'S STORY

Part of the problem was that our relationship looked just fine— from the outside. So if I were to tell someone how awful it was, how hurt I was, how there were all these illusions—they wouldn't believe me. They'd think I was the crazy one, and she would support that idea. Anyway, telling other people would be embarrassing. What, I can't deal with a relationship? But there's truth in that. People warned me about her and I thought they were crazy. It's so hard to admit they were right. I made a big mistake!

MELINDA'S STORY

I grew up in a narcissistic family situation. I've tried to get away, and failed. I've learned that if you live with a narcissist, no matter who she or he is, they'll do everything they can to keep you there. It's almost impossible to escape. I can't just say, "I don't want to be with you anymore." It doesn't work. Escape is the only way, and that's really hard. Everyone thinks my parents are this wonderful couple, and in public that's how they look. They do charity work, socialize, they dress nice, and look and sound great. But it's an act. And they have everyone convinced I'm this sick, lazy, crazy person! Everyone's disgusted by me because of what they've been told. I'm alone. Totally alone. My family has ruined my life, especially by spreading lies about the kind of person I am, and doing it very well! How could the people who are supposed to love and support you be so horrible? I'm starting to think my only option is to leave the country!

The foregoing stories illustrate some of the traits of narcissism and the nature of narcissistic abuse. If you've been in situations similar to these, you can easily identify with the feelings of confusion, fear, and devastation the scenarios can produce. For most of us, the desperate need to understand exactly why these twisted conflicts are so disturbing leads to a search for some solid answers. The first question for most of us is "What is a narcissist?"

DEFINING NARCISSISM

When you Google the word *narcissist*, you are flooded with information. For many people suffering with a narcissist, the initial exposure to solid information and definitions is transformative. If we can label and define the narcissist, as well as the tactics used, then we can begin to mount a defense, move forward, and eventually move on and move past the horror. It's comforting to know that the effects of narcissistic abuse are quite real, because it's a validation of our own experiences, and, just as important, reading others' accounts is a sure sign that we are not alone.

This section will explore some of the many terms used to define narcissism both clinically (by psychologists and mental health professionals) and socially (by knowledgeable leaders in the field who do not happen to have academic degrees).

Let's begin with the "official" definition of narcissism. For definitive clinical diagnostic criteria, mental health professionals generally refer to the DSM-5, the *Diagnostic and Statistical Manual of Mental Disorders* published by the American Psychiatric Association. Narcissism is a personality disorder, one of several including borderline personality disorder, antisocial personality disorder, and histrionic personality disorder. There are a few qualities that overlap among these disorders, and although we are focusing on narcissism, it's very possible that your pathological partner also fits into one of these alternate categories. Even if the narcissist is not "diagnosable" and does not meet all the criteria for a psychiatric diagnosis, he or she is still fully capable of utterly ruining your life.

The hallmarks of narcissistic personality disorder (NPD) are grandiosity, a lack of empathy for other people, and a need for admiration. People with this condition are frequently described as arrogant, self-centered, manipulative, and demanding. They may also have grandiose fantasies and be convinced that they deserve special treatment. These characteristics are evident in numerous contexts, such as at work and in relationships, though the narcissist may save his or her worst traits just for you. People with NPD often try to associate with other people they believe are unique or gifted in some way, which can enhance their own self-esteem. They tend to seek excessive admiration and attention and have difficulty tolerating criticism. In order to get maximum attention, they will sometimes take credit for work or achievements that others, namely you, have actually accomplished.

Individuals with narcissistic personality disorder, according to the DSM-5, exhibit five or more of the following:

1. A grandiose sense of self-importance
2. Preoccupation with fantasies of unlimited success, power, brilliance, beauty, or ideal love

3. Belief that one is special and can only be understood by or associate with special people or institutions
4. A need for excessive admiration
5. A sense of entitlement (to special treatment)
6. Exploitation of others
7. A lack of empathy
8. Envy of others or the belief that one is the object of envy
9. Arrogant, haughty behavior or attitudes

Individuals with NPD can be easily stung by criticism or defeat and may react with disdain or anger—but social withdrawal or the false appearance of humility may also follow.

A sense of entitlement, disregard for other people, and other aspects of NPD will damage relationships. While a person with NPD may be a high achiever, the disorder can also have a negative impact on performance (due to, for instance, one's sensitivity to criticism).

The DSM-5 also captures the differences between healthy and unhealthy personalities. According to the definition of personality disorders, the key elements are as follows:

1. A personality disorder is an enduring pattern of inner experience and behavior. This pattern manifests in disturbances in two or more of the following areas:

    a. Thinking
    b. Feeling
    c. Interpersonal relationships
    d. Impulse control

2. This pattern deviates markedly from cultural norms and expectations.
3. This pattern is pervasive and inflexible. It is almost always present and does not vary.

4. It is stable over time. In other words, it's permanent.
5. It leads to distress or impairment. [It also leads to distress and impairment for others!]

The DSM-5 identifies and describes ten specific personality disorders. These diagnoses represent ten specific enduring patterns of thought, feelings, and behavior. However, each of these ten patterns can be distilled to four core features of personality disorders:

1. Rigid, extreme, and distorted thinking patterns (thoughts)
2. Problematic emotional response patterns (feelings)
3. Impulse control problems (behavior)
4. Significant interpersonal problems (behavior)

You can expect any or all of the following from an individual with a personality disorder:

1. NEGATIVE AFFECT (the opposite is emotional stability): Emotional lability, anxiousness, separation anxiety, hostility, perseveration
2. DETACHMENT: Withdrawal, intimacy avoidance, anhedonia (lack of genuine enjoyment), depressivity, restricted affect (limited emotional range), suspiciousness
3. ANTAGONISM: Manipulativeness, deceitfulness, grandiosity, attention seeking, callousness, hostility
4. DISINHIBITION: Irresponsibility, impulsivity, distractibility, risk-taking, rigid perfectionism
5. PSYCHOTISM: Unusual beliefs and experiences, eccentricity, cognitive and perceptual dysregulation

That is quite a cauldron of relationship-destroying features! You may also hear some of the personality disorders referred to as "cluster B" disorders. Cluster B is known as the dramatic, emotional, and erratic cluster. Disorders in this group share the problems of impulse control and emotional regulation. They include antisocial personality disorder, borderline personality disorder, and narcissistic personality disorder.

ANTISOCIAL PERSONALITY DISORDER

Antisocial personality disorder is characterized by a pervasive pattern of disregard for the rights of other people that often manifests as hostility and/or aggression. Deceit and manipulation are also central features. In many cases, hostile-aggressive and deceitful behaviors first appear during childhood. These children may hurt or torment animals or people. They may engage in hostile acts such as bullying or intimidating others. They may have a reckless disregard for property, such as by setting fires. They often engage in deceit, theft, and other serious violations of standard rules of conduct. They frequently act on impulsive urges without considering the consequences.

Persons with antisocial personality disorder typically do not experience genuine remorse for the harm they cause others. However, they can become quite adept at feigning remorse when it is in their best interest. They take little or no responsibility for their actions. In fact, they will often blame their victims for "causing" their wrong actions or for being deserving of their own fate. The aggressive features of this personality disorder make it stand out among others because individuals with this disorder take a singular toll on society.

BORDERLINE PERSONALITY DISORDER

People with borderline personality disorder tend to experience intense and unstable emotions and moods that can shift fairly quickly. They generally have a hard time calming down once they have become upset. As a result, they frequently have angry outbursts and engage in impulsive behaviors such as substance abuse, risky sexual liaisons, self-injury, overspending, or binge eating. These behaviors often function to soothe them in the short term but harm them in the longer term.

People with borderline personality disorder tend to see the world in polarized, oversimplified, all-or-nothing terms. They apply their harsh either/or judgments to others and to themselves, and their perceptions of themselves and others may quickly vacillate between all good and all bad. This tendency leads to an unstable sense of self, so that persons with this disorder tend to have a hard time being consistent.

These individuals frequently change careers, relationships, life goals, or residences. Quite often these radical changes occur without any warning or advance preparation. Clearly, the person with borderline personality disorder, with its combination of distorted thought patterns, black-and-white thinking, intense and underregulated emotions, and poor impulse control, is practically destined to wreak havoc on any interpersonal relationship.

While perusing literature and Internet sources, you may also come across the term "dark triad," which refers to a trio of negative personality traits—narcissism, Machiavellianism, and psychopathy—that share some common malevolent features.

People with these traits tend to be callous and manipulative, willing to do or say practically anything to get their way. They have an inflated view of themselves and are often shameless about self-promotion. These individuals are likely to be impulsive and may engage in dangerous behavior—in some cases, even committing crimes—without any regard for how their actions affect others.

While many researchers consider psychopathy, narcissism, and Machiavellianism to be three distinct traits with overlapping characteristics, others believe the commonalities suggest an underlying personality construct that has yet to be fully understood.

Machiavellianism is not a mental health diagnosis; rather, it's a personality trait describing a manipulative individual who deceives and tricks others to achieve goals. The name comes from the sixteenth-century diplomat, philosopher, and author Niccolò Machiavelli and is based on his political philosophy. This philosophy required an effective leader to be more concerned with personal reputation than the needs of others and to be willing to act unscrupulously at the right times. To Machiavelli, dissent of any kind was to be stopped because it is the root of betrayal. Some evidence suggests that, of the dark traits, Machiavellianism is most closely tied to high intelligence. Having a "high Mach" means that one behaves in a highly manipulative manner and is well aware of what he or she is crafting.

Most researchers consider psychopathy—a trait characterized by a lack of both empathy and remorse—to be the darkest of the dark triad (whose three traits often seem to coexist in psychopaths). Psychopaths generally cause more harm to individuals and to society than do narcissists or Machiavellians. "Psychopath" is not a mental health diagnosis; the disorder that most closely represents it in the DSM is antisocial personality disorder.

It's not known what causes narcissistic personality disorder. As with personality development and other mental health disorders, the cause is complex. The origin of NPD is likely to include dysfunctions in the following:

Environment—mismatches in parent-child relationships, with either excessive adoration or excessive criticism that is poorly attuned to the child's experience

Genetics—inherited characteristics

Neurobiology—the connection between the brain, behavior, and thinking

The most recent research available actually de-emphasizes adverse childhood experiences and irrational thought patterns in favor of genetics and built-in neurobiology as the likely origin of narcissism. Such research underscores the view that the narcissist will not "get better" as a result of treatment and that therapy for a narcissist is quite likely to fail.

Narcissistic personality disorder affects more males than females, and it often begins in the teens or early adulthood. Keep in mind that, although some children show narcissistic traits, this may simply be typical of their age and doesn't mean they'll go on to develop narcissistic personality disorder.

THE WHIRLWIND OF NARCISSISM

Narcissists maintain an atmosphere of chaos and conflict. The following are more perspectives on how it feels to be in a relationship with a narcissistic partner.

THE NEED TO DECEIVE

In her book *When Evil Is a Pretty Face*, Zari Ballard describes narcissists as having not only the ability to deceive, which is common to us all, but also both an eagerness and a necessity to deceive, which the narcissist's target often experiences as bone-deep betrayal. Unlike the typical insensitive or self-centered person, the narcissist shifts between idolizing, manipulating, devaluing, and (either by appearance or actually) discarding. The effect can be dizzying and demoralizing.

The narcissist's agenda is pathological. The target is expected to be always available and utterly devoted, tolerant, and willing to serve the narcissist. Rarely, if ever, are any of these responsibilities reciprocated.

Questioning the narcissist's agenda or behavior brings about swift, often devastating, reprisals.

Narcissists are professionals at holding grudges but are equally proficient at appearing normal, responsible, and innocent. What at first appears to be a desirable relationship can be swallowed whole by the target having to cope with narcissistic behavior. The narcissist will do just about anything for the spotlight, to be the all-consuming star of every circumstance and relationship, and will embarrass, cajole, denigrate, lie, and punish in service of this goal.

DENIAL AND EVASION

In Jackson MacKenzie's book *Psychopath Free*, manipulative behavior is described as often hidden, never admitted, and often blamed on the target, who is deemed too sensitive or immature to cope with such normal interaction. Expecting empathy from "how would you feel if you were in my shoes" protestations engenders a blank stare, a tantrum, or worse. Vulnerability is exploited. Targets learn to hide their feelings.

LIES AND CONFLICT

Your love and adoration are expected, with none consistently given in return. Lies become the norm. Catching the narcissist in a lie leads to ever more ridiculous excuses, and avalanches of blame. It may sometimes seem as if the liar expected to be caught—narcissists revel in the conflict, where attention can be focused on your mistakes and flaws.

INVALIDATION AND CONTEMPT

Their selfishness is breathtaking and hard to fathom—so much so that being in a relationship with a narcissist can lead one to question one's own sanity. Did that really happen? Did they really do that? Life seems like a bad dream. No one else sees what you see in this person, who reacts to any suggestion of their bearing responsibility or accountability with first subtle, then blatant, attacks on your own. So you find yourself scrolling back through their social media accounts, playing detective, looking for some kind of validation for your perception of this crazy behavior, thinking you'll know it when you see it. Once you find yourself recording conversations, checking security cameras, or going through the narcissist's social media posts, there is nothing left that's healthy in the relationship. It's done.

PUBLIC AND PRIVATE FACES

One reason your relationship feels crazy is that your partner seemed so sane at first. Not only sane, but wonderful! He or she not only knew what love was but was obsessed with overwhelming you with it. Looking back, of course, the fact that this flattery and love bombing was a tactic to draw you in may be only too apparent, and yet, even in hindsight, it remains seductive. The relationship's insanity is also difficult to accept because this seemingly normal person, who may be successful in a chosen field, well educated, well dressed, and in all appearances an achiever, behaves in ways that are at once utterly unreasonable and unacceptable. Anyone would agree! Yet no one can see it but you!

CONCLUSIONS

Being in a relationship—any relationship—with a narcissist is dangerous. Leaving one is challenging. The narcissist may lead you to believe that he or she is the one who is leaving, which is either a tactic to elicit attention or achieve a goal, or evidence that the narcissist has gained all he or she could from the relationship and is ready to discard you. If that is the case, consider yourself lucky, pack your bags, and go home. The narcissist will want to choose the terms on which the relationship will end.

You may believe that, because you are educated, you are immune or somehow able to transcend the narcissist's behavior. You may be a professional speech therapist, an attorney, a medical doctor or other educated, savvy, or experienced expert, but the narcissist is a professional of sorts too—a professional narcissist. Would you survive a boxing match with a professional fighter? Could you beat an Olympic runner in a race? It is not reasonable to expect to beat a narcissist at his or her own game. You won't win. They are the experts. The only way to win with a narcissist is to leave the game. Disengage.

People you are close to may try to convince you that you are better off remaining where you are, that it is not worth the aggravation and complexity of a breakup or divorce. Some may even suggest that you can't do it, that you can never leave. It's not true. You can escape. And you will.

QUESTION: In your professional opinion, can a narcissist ever "get better"?

DR. FRED

The very short answer is no. They seem impervious to therapy. In fact, it's counterproductive to be in therapy with a narcissist, sometimes to the point of being dangerous. They are fully capable of influencing a professional therapist, commandeering each session and very effectively "throwing you under the bus." Some recent studies indicate that only about 2 percent of people with personality disorders improve after a full course of psychotherapy!

DR. ROBIN

No, because they don't realize that they have issues or see themselves clearly. They project their weaknesses and self-hatred onto others with whom they have intimate relationships. For change to occur, people need to embrace their flaws and want to do the work on themselves to make positive changes. Narcissists are incapable of this. Narcissists think that "crazy" people need therapists, certainly not them.

3

The Tragic Story of Narcissus and Echo (and Other Narcissists in Literature)

The story of Echo and Narcissus can be found in more than one ancient source, including book three of Ovid's *Metamorphoses*. In the story, Narcissus encounters Echo, a mountain nymph known as an oread, who falls in love with him at first sight. She follows him, and, sensing her presence, Narcissus calls out, "Who is there?" He hears his question echoed back to him by the nymph: "Who is there?"

When Echo reveals herself to Narcissus and reaches for him, he rejects her, telling her to leave him alone. Heartbroken, Echo spends the rest of her life wandering the valleys and glens, able only to speak words spoken first by another. Eventually, nothing is left of Echo but an echo. This is an apt analogy of how it feels to be the victim of a narcissist. Empty, hollow, depleted, merely an echo of your former self.

In the myth, Nemesis, the goddess of revenge, learns what happened between Narcissus and Echo and punishes him one summer day by luring him to a pond. When Narcissus leans over the water, he sees a reflection of himself in the prime of his youth. Unaware that he is seeing his own reflection, he falls in love with it. Obsessed with his image, he cannot leave the spot. When he realizes his love will be forever unrequited, he is melted away by the fires of his own passion, until all that is left of him is a white and gold flower, known today as the narcissus, a variety of daffodil. Ovid's version of the myth was composed about two thousand years ago, yet it accurately describes the modern narcissist and the devastation associated with narcissistic abuse.

Other versions of the myth also end badly for Narcissus. In one version, attributed to the poet Parthenius of Nicaea, a devastated Narcissus kills himself. In another, attributed to a contemporary of Ovid's, Narcissus also dies by suicide. In each version, Narcissus is so obsessed with his own image and so in love with himself that he would rather die than live without a love that only he himself could fulfill.

BUT SHOULDN'T WE LOVE OURSELVES?

We have all heard the suggestion, either from therapists or from self-help media, that we should love ourselves. Taken at face value, loving what we see in the mirror, or in a reflective body of water for that matter, is not a bad thing. Self-hatred and poor self-esteem are not emotionally healthy. So what's wrong with Narcissus? Wasn't he just loving himself? Narcissus did not merely love himself; he fell in love with himself, and therein lies the difference.

If the narcissist were alone, like Narcissus early in the story, the damage would be minimal. Like Narcissus, the narcissist would look in the mirror, swoon, and possibly be done with it. Damage would be limited to the narcissist himself. But Narcissus did not remain alone. His self-love was devastating to Echo.

In discussing narcissism, so much is said about Narcissus. How appropriate. Narcissists are always the focus! Yet consider the plight of poor Echo. In loving Narcissus, she has lost her identity and become nothing but a fleeting echo of him. Life with narcissists emulates the myth; those who love them are doomed to lose themselves in their magnetic aura. Everything in proximity to the narcissist becomes a reflection of him. If we were to learn more about his life, we would likely find that others echo or reflect him as well: his family, coworkers, friends. When dealing with a narcissist there is no other, as there is no room in his or her attention for anyone else. There are only wonderful (of course!) aspects of him that are reflected in those around him. The closer one is to the narcissist, the fainter one's own light shines. For those unfortunate enough to be closest to the narcissist, there can be little left but an echo of the narcissist. One loses one's identity entirely.

More to the point, those in proximity to the narcissist are in grave danger. The origin story only goes so far and presents only one scenario. History does not provide us with the details of Narcissus's life and relationships beyond what is included in the myths, but one can imagine his day-to-day life with a significant other, a parent, a child, a contemporary. He would be so captivated with himself that he would have no regard for anyone else in his life. We have only to imagine Narcissus with others to envision the damage he would do.

The narcissist engages in far more and far worse than self-love. The narcissist controls others—locking the lover, child, sibling, parent, employee, or coworker in a death grip that encompasses emotions, behaviors, finances, and more. One is expected to be utterly devoted to the narcissist in every way. Dare to take time for yourself, to treat yourself to a special purchase or food, a friendship, a concert, or just about anything that does not include and focus on the narcissist, and you risk being seen as a direct threat. No one holds a grudge like a narcissist. Yes, they are obsessed with themselves, but that obsession is reflected not in a pool of water but in self-serving, dangerous behavior. Arranging others' lives to suit themselves is their expertise. They are professionals. Their specialty is rooting out disrespect, and finding it everywhere since no one can live up to their expectations. Their retribution and retaliation skills are fiercely and finely honed, even when there was no real injury to them to begin with.

With narcissists, you are only safe when you are alone and serving them. Your obsession with them must be nearly equal to their own obsession with themselves. They believe they deserve nothing less. You are allowed to love no one else, least of all yourself. The narcissist expects to be served, and it is your duty to serve, though it is rarely appreciated or reciprocated. They know your fears and weaknesses because not only have they studied them thoroughly, they helped create them in the first place. They can push your buttons because they helped install them. And they know how to use your fears to keep you in line, to keep you serving them, to ensure you love no one else, including yourself. Living with a narcissist is, quite literally, a nightmare from which you can never be allowed to leave or wake up.

If we were to meet the real Narcissus and have access to his life outside the environs of the myth, away from the pool, we might see why he is alone and so captivated by his own reflection. Everyone else took the nearest chariot and spirited themselves away.

THE NARCISSIST'S FATE

In *Echoes of Narcissus*, edited by Lieve Spaas, we learn that Narcissus was the product of a rape. The blue-water nymph Liriope was raped by the river god Cephisus. In Ovid's myth, Narcissus is sixteen years old, neither boy nor man. He behaves from both standpoints, as a child and as a grown man. He has been on a hunt for a stag, interpreted as an "unconscious search for himself," when he stops to drink from water that reflects his image. This inspires desire and love for that beautiful face. Once he realizes that the image he loves is his own, he thinks himself split in two, in love with his own double, and wishes himself whole again.

Echo misinterprets Narcissus's loving exclamations, which are meant for his own image, as being directed toward her. She throws her arms around his neck, but Narcissus rejects her, saying he would die "before I yield to you." She echoes the sentiment back to him with "I yield to you." Tragically, we do wind up yielding to the narcissist, not always initially understanding why we do so.

Erich Fromm explains that narcissists are unable to love, because it requires a selflessness quite beyond their abilities. The world exists only to serve the narcissist, and when it does not, it is rejected. Like their namesake, narcissists are forever metaphorically gazing at themselves in the mirror. The needs and loves of others do not interest them; they feel pleasure only in forever taking, and cannot fathom the dignity or integrity of others.

Another textbook example of the narcissist in classic literature is Dorian Gray. In Oscar Wilde's *The Picture of Dorian Gray*, Gray's "mirror" is his painted portrait, which ages in place of his actual body, as a result, appropriately, of a deal he makes with the Devil himself. Gray gets to remain forever young and beautiful. His reaction upon seeing his own image is one of joy and, quite possibly, lust. He sees himself and draws back, his cheeks flushed with pleasure. As with

Ovid's Narcissus, the reader is warned that beauty does not last and that "what the gods give, they quickly take away."

Both stories can be read as cautionary tales about the inevitable pain caused by self-obsession. In time, we all lose our youth and beauty and become "hollow-cheeked and dull-eyed," and we may suffer. Gray's portrait reveals his character. As he indulges his narcissism, his portrait bears visual testament to his immorality and displays the ravages of time and avarice. Like Narcissus, who forever sees his image in hell in the river Styx, Dorian Gray is in a hell of his own making, via his own self-obsessed vices. Ultimately, Gray's self-loathing drives him to suicide, matching some versions of the Narcissus narrative.

Ovid's Narcissus and Echo myth and *The Picture of Dorian Gray* both portray classic narcissistic self-obsession and the downfall that inevitably follows. Despite their awareness of their pain and its causes, neither character is capable of change. Narcissus remains forever self-obsessed yet unfulfilled. Dorian Gray is devastated by the hideous changes in his portrait and hides it away to avoid having to see it.

ECHOISM: FORGETTING WHO WE ARE

Echoism, according to a blog post on Healthline.com, has been referred to as "the other side of narcissism." The term refers to the nymph who was so infatuated with Narcissus that she became, literally, an echo. Her own personality, her self, was subsumed by her adoration of Narcissus. Cursed by Hera, she is left unable to speak, except to repeat the last words spoken by others. When a narcissist finds someone who will supply their desperate need for attention and adoration, that individual may lose his or her sense of self and become a pale "echo" of the narcissist, echoing his opinions, ideas, and perceptions while losing their own.

The term "echoist" was coined by clinical psychologist and expert on narcissism Craig Malkin, PhD. Central to being an echoist is a fear of seeming narcissistic. An echoist fears being the center of attention or a burden to others. Such individuals tend to be warmhearted to the point of over-giving and under-receiving. They are self-effacing and overly modest. People who exhibit traits of echoism tend to be vulnerable to abuse from dark personality types, including narcissists and various types of psychopaths.

Echoists avoid any (real or imagined) spotlight. Even subtly acknowledging their accomplishments or needs makes them feel selfish, undeserving, or guilty—they're constantly on the lookout in case they appear narcissistic.

If you find yourself identifying as an echoist, it's important to make an honest inventory of what you have accomplished. What are your best traits? What are you proud of? How would you want to be introduced to a stranger? Make a list of everything awesome you've done, what you've added or subtracted from your life, mental breakthroughs, improvements, and so forth. It doesn't matter if you judge them as being too small, silly, or easy. All that matters is that they mean something to you. Know that you are allowed to have healthy boundaries and that you can assert them gracefully.

There is a lot of overlap between the traits of an echoist and those of a person with low self-esteem, low self-worth, depression, or trauma. Chapter 8 covers things you can do to heal and recover.

QUESTION: What were a few things that first attracted you to the narcissist in your life?

DR. FRED

With a narcissist, there is always a thrilling, intriguing opening chapter. They are interesting, dynamic, and a little wild. Mine was always suggesting new things to try, new places to go, always pushing the limits. So I would have to say a sense of adventure and a high degree of creativity attracted me to my narcissist. Unfortunately, a narcissist will eventually use all that energy and creativity to destroy you.

DR. ROBIN

Everything! He was so charismatic, attentive, and interesting. We were friends for years and little did I know how much he was studying me and manipulating me into creating this fantasy relationship. I was naïve and trusting. He was a textbook vulnerable narcissist with a great sob story, and, being the good girl and fixer that I was, I willingly entered his web of lies and deceit.

4

Literary Interlude

ALICE AND DOROTHY: HEROINES WHO DEFEATED THE NARCISSISTS WHO WERE DETERMINED TO DESTROY THEM

Alice was a well-educated Victorian-era English girl. Dorothy was a farm-raised rural Kansas girl. Each was unexpectedly thrown into a fantasy world, completely alone, where vicious antagonists repeatedly attempted to confuse, belittle, and even terminate them. There are many appropriate metaphors for aspects of narcissistic relationships in these works, including the now well-known term "flying monkeys." We are referring, of course, to *Alice's Adventures in Wonderland* by Lewis Carroll and *The Wonderful Wizard of Oz* by L. Frank Baum.

When you meet a narcissist, it is, indeed, like falling down a rabbit hole. "Alice had not a moment to think about stopping herself before she found herself falling down a very deep well." The love bombing in a narcissistic relationship can be like a dream, and we do not realize, in the whirlwind, that there is a grand manipulation going on. "'Well!' thought Alice to herself, 'after such a fall as this, I shall think nothing

of tumbling down stairs!'" How quickly we grow accustomed to the level of abuse and absurdity.

Throughout Alice's adventure she is belittled, purposely confused, insulted, put on trial, and threatened with beheading! Her body image is distorted as she grows and shrinks after sipping from the "Drink Me" bottle and nibbling on some magic mushrooms. Characters are not what or who they seem, often refusing to answer legitimate questions. Although the story is whimsically written, Alice is portrayed as being in very real distress.

The Caterpillar in particular, like the narcissist in a relationship, has Alice literally questioning her own identity: "'Who are YOU?' said the Caterpillar. Alice replied, rather shyly, 'I—I hardly know, sir, just at present—at least I know who I WAS when I got up this morning, but I think I must have been changed several times since then.'" And further, when the Caterpillar says, "Explain yourself!" Alice replies, "I can't explain MYSELF, I'm afraid, sir, because I'm not myself, you see."

Alice, like a person caught in a narcissist's web, begins to feel "quite mad" (meaning crazy in this case, not angry). The ultimate scene involves the Cheshire Cat, itself nothing but a smiling mask, guiding Alice to the Mad Tea Party; a better analogy to a narcissist's circle of cronies is hard to imagine! It's reminiscent of meeting a narcissist's family for the first time:

"How do you know I'm mad?" said Alice.

"You must be," said the Cat, "or you wouldn't have come here."

"But I don't want to go among mad people," Alice remarked.

"Oh, you can't help that," said the Cat: "we're all mad here. I'm mad. You're mad."

MEETING THE NARCISSIST'S FAMILY
FOR THE FIRST TIME

The Cheshire Cat's lingering grin is often compared to the "evil smirk" of a narcissist. After leaving the Mad Tea Party, Alice is further harassed and belittled by the March Hare, the Mad Hatter, and a host of other devious characters. It's gaslighting on a grand scale. Croquet mallets turn into flamingos, a game ball turns into a hedgehog. Turtles are "mock," and a cat dissolves into a floating, ghostly grin. It is, in fact, enough to drive a person mad.

Along the way, Alice demonstrates her empathetic tendencies. She volunteers to take care of an infant (that later turns out to be a pig), she helps defend the Mad Hatter who is accused in court of stealing, and she feels sorry for the fate of various characters, all the while being threatened by the Red Queen, who wants to decapitate her!

The only way out, as with leaving a narcissistic relationship, is to see through the deception and wake up from the nightmare. Alice resolutely defies the twisted logic and falsehoods thrown at her. For example, in the final trial scene, the King claims that Rule #42 is the "oldest rule in the book," and when Alice defiantly states, "Then it should be Rule #1," the King is taken aback. When the courtroom turns violently against her, Alice eventually exclaims, "You are nothing but a pack of cards!" and escapes Wonderland by knocking over the "jury box" and brushing away the attacking deck. Lewis Carroll surely intended to satirize the oppressive nature of Victorian society, but there are many inspirational moments for someone about to leave an emotionally abusive relationship.

"Who cares for you?" said Alice. (She has grown to her full size by this time.) "You're nothing but a pack of cards!"

THE WONDERFUL WIZARD OF OZ

Or maybe not so wonderful. Dorothy, in L. Frank Baum's classic, is also literally whisked away into a land of wonder where a wicked witch harbors an unreasonable grudge and will do anything to exact revenge. Here, too, Dorothy is an empathetic character.

"I'm not feeling well," said the Scarecrow, with a smile, "for it is very tedious being perched up here night and day to scare away crows."

"Can't you get down?" asked Dorothy.

"If you will please take away the pole I shall be greatly obliged to you."

Dorothy reached up both arms and lifted the figure off the pole, for, being stuffed with straw, it was quite light.

Next, Dorothy assists the Tin Man.

"What can I do for you?" she inquired softly, for she was moved by the sad voice in which the man spoke.

"Get an oil-can and oil my joints," he answered.

After she helps, he says, "I might have stood there always if you had not come along, so you have certainly saved my life."

Later, Dorothy helps the Cowardly Lion. Although she is the one who was transported to this land, she winds up in the service of others.

Like Alice with her "Drink Me" bottle and her magic mushroom, Dorothy is also drugged, this time by a field of deadly poppies governed by the Wicked Witch.

They found themselves in the midst of a great meadow of poppies. Now it is well known that when there are many of these flowers together, their odor is so powerful that anyone who breathes it falls asleep, and if the sleeper is not carried away from the scent of the flowers, he sleeps on and on forever.

"The smell of the flowers is killing us all. I myself can scarcely keep my eyes open, and the dog is asleep already."

An analogy can be drawn to the alluring intoxication of initial love bombing and the charm of a true narcissist.

The great Oz, at first, is the ultimate narcissist. Grandiose, but hiding behind a mask. His Emerald City glistens in green only because all the citizens are forced to wear green-tinted glasses. As with the narcissist, nothing is what it seems.

"You see, Oz is a Great Wizard, and can take on any form he wishes. So that some say he looks like a bird; and some say he looks like an elephant; and some say he looks like a cat. To others he appears as a beautiful fairy, or a brownie, or in any other form that pleases him. But who the real Oz is, when he is in his own form, no living person can tell."

An amazing description of the manipulative narcissist.

"I never grant favors without some return," said Oz.

That's a profound description! There are always strings attached to narcissistic favors.

"I thought you asked Dorothy to kill the Witch," said the Scarecrow, in surprise.

"So I did," [said Oz.] "I don't care who kills her. But until she is dead I will not grant your wish. Now go, and do not seek me again until you have earned the brains you so greatly desire."

And, finally, that brings us to the infamous "Winged Monkeys," themselves slaves to the narcissistic Wicked Witch:

There was, in her cupboard, a Golden Cap, with a circle of diamonds and rubies running round it. Whoever owned it

could call upon the Winged Monkeys, who would obey any order they were given . . .

. . . The sky was darkened, and a low rumbling sound was heard in the air. There was a rushing of many wings, a great chattering and laughing, and the sun came out of the dark sky to show the Wicked Witch surrounded by a crowd of monkeys, each with a pair of immense and powerful wings on his shoulders.

The narcissist has released her corrupt cronies and loyal worshippers. This image is so clear that it has remained the most definitive visual to illustrate a narcissist's evil entourage for over a hundred and twenty years!

Here, Baum depicts the Witch's gaslighting, illustrating what every narcissist is probably contemplating with his or her own manipulative antics.

But the wicked creature was very cunning, and she finally thought of a trick that would give her what she wanted. She placed a bar of iron in the middle of the kitchen floor, and then by her magic arts made the iron invisible to human eyes. So that when Dorothy walked across the floor she stumbled over the bar, not being able to see it, and fell at full length. She was not much hurt, but in her fall one of the Silver Shoes came off; and before she could reach it, the Witch had snatched it away and put it on her own skinny foot. The wicked woman was greatly pleased with the success of her trick.

Dorothy persists, however, unafraid of the deception.

This made Dorothy so very angry that she picked up the bucket of water that stood near and dashed it over the Witch, wetting her from head to foot. Instantly the wicked woman gave a loud cry of fear, and then, as Dorothy looked at her in wonder, the Witch began to shrink and fall away.

After picking out the silver shoe, which was all that was left of the old woman, she cleaned and dried it with a cloth, and put it on her foot again.

Dorothy's stunning realization that her abusers are not as strong as they seemed grants her clarity and strength. They are destroyed by the simple revelation of who they really are. Deep inside, the narcissist is as inconsequential as a pack of cards, and as weak as a melted mess on the floor, killed by common water.

And, of course, the Wizard of Oz does not keep his promise of returning Dorothy to her rural home. He provides a great example of future faking. Oz sends Dorothy on a life-threatening mission to do the work he is too cowardly to accomplish, only to renege on the deal. The Kansas farm girl, being far braver, smarter, and more wonderful than the wizard himself, gets the job done. Dorothy must get home on her own.

Even the Emerald City is a complete illusion, as is the entire world of the narcissist.

"Just to amuse myself, and keep the good people busy," said Oz, "I ordered them to build this City, and my Palace; and they did it all willingly and well. Then I thought, as the country was so green and beautiful, I would call it the Emerald City; and to make the name fit better I put green spectacles on all the people, so that everything they saw was green."

"But isn't everything here green?" asked Dorothy.

"No more than in any other city," replied Oz; "but when you wear green spectacles, why of course everything you see looks green to you. But my people have worn green glasses on their eyes so long that most of them think it really is an Emerald City."

Even on her journey back to Kansas, Dorothy is more concerned about her Auntie Em's well-being than her own.

"My greatest wish now," she added, "is to get back to Kansas, for Aunt Em will surely think something dreadful has happened to me, and that will make her put on mourning; and unless the crops are better this year than they were last, I am sure Uncle Henry cannot afford it."

Great lessons from a couple of literature's most famous and wonderful girls.

QUESTION: What was the most influential song, book, website, or resource that helped with your own journey away from the narcissist?

DR. FRED

There is a great social media source called Shrink4Men that focuses on men who are in narcissistic relationships. It was created by Dr. Tara Palmatier. Not only did her books and other websites help me, but she was my private therapist for a brief time. Her book *Say Goodbye to Crazy* focuses mainly on how a woman can deal with a man's crazy ex-wife, but it helped me recognize my own situation too. Two songs helped me through the process: "Don't Come around Here No More" by Tom Petty and the more recent "Sweet But Psycho" by Ava Max.

DR. ROBIN

When I was in the thick of it (and those who are reading this book know exactly what I mean!), I started to Google some words that described what the narcissist was doing (e.g., lying, staying out all night). A YouTube video by Angie Atkinson on narcissistic abuse popped up, and at that point my healing journey began. I started watching YouTube videos on narcissistic abuse and codependency. I also began going to conferences, learning, and reading as much as I could about personality disorders.

5

The Narcissist's Arsenal

TERMS OF ENTRAPMENT
(A GLOSSARY)

Narcissists seem to consult the same playbook for tactics to feed their addiction to attention, yet differences do sometimes emerge. Some exhibit overt narcissistic behavior and seem to be proud of their narcissism. Others are covert narcissists and may be harder to detect. All narcissists have an arsenal of weaponry and a bevy of tactics with which to achieve their goal of attracting, capturing, and holding on to their prey.

Becoming familiar with the vocabulary of narcissism is the first step to empowerment. When we can name and identify something, we can understand it better, feel less alone, and begin to break free. This chapter will cover all the terms, tactics, and techniques that you can expect from a narcissist.

•   •   •

1. SOURCE/SUPPLY

A narcissist is like a vampire who needs a fresh supply of blood, in the form of attention and control, every night in order to survive. Or think of the narcissist as an addict, whose drugs are the ego-feeding, subservient, submissive, dominated behaviors he or she feeds on. In order to feel secure, narcissists need approval and admiration; they need people to revolve around them as a planet does around a shining sun. An individual who is in the clutches of a narcissist is his or her "source" or "supply." Everything that supports the narcissist's pathology is supply.

The words *supply* and *source* are often used interchangeably with the word *target*. We are avoiding the word *victim*, not because those affected by the narcissist are not victims; they are. We avoid the word *victim* because we want to empower those affected by narcissists, rather than the opposite. People affected by narcissists need not see themselves as passive victims when they can actively determine the course of their relationships. People in relationships with narcissists can end those relationships, albeit often with the help of a professional. They have within their grasp the means to escape the narcissist and to be free of the effects of the narcissistic relationship.

Preston Ni at *Psychology Today* defines narcissistic supply as "a form of psychological addiction and dependency, where the narcissist requires (demands) constant importance, 'special treatment,' validation, and/or appeasement in order to feel good about him or herself." Narcissists strive to find, create, and maintain circumstances that will ensure their ongoing access to such supply. They seek complete control.

2. GROOMING

Just as we all want love, we also want positive attention. Narcissists are master manipulators, and one of their primary weapons is grooming. Grooming is the technique of systematically "prepping" the intended target. Narcissists entice their target with ever-increasing favors, compliments, or presents that are carefully chosen to have an emotional impact. Grooming can also take the form of consistently favorable comments on social media posts. Rather than coerce, connive, or bully—any of which a narcissist might resort to later on—the narcissist grooms the target into willing compliance with love bombing, gift-giving, future faking (a.k.a. false promises), and outright lies.

Narcissists store in their arsenals a variety of weapons that have similar functions, each with the goal of creating compliance. Once achieved, compliance can be a doorway to sex, access to assets, returned affection, and more. Grooming is often aimed at the target's insecurities. For instance, if a woman is insecure about her weight, the narcissist might comment that she looks thin one day, too thin another day, and overweight on a third day, leaving her confused, bewildered, and more easily controlled. Such comments might be spread over hours, days, weeks, or longer. Narcissists sometimes choose already insecure or codependent people as their target, making the grooming process that much easier. But they may be just as likely to choose a strong, successful, self-assured person to target. That person's eventual fall to ruin will be more dramatic, more of an "achievement" for the narcissist.

Grooming tactics might include expressing interest in the target's life, sharing their own (claimed) vulnerabilities, acting as though they are attracted to the target, or doing the target favors. They perpetually collect vulnerabilities for later use. Any insecurity the target shares will be cataloged, sorted, and stored in the narcissist's arsenal of psychological weapons. But it won't stop there. The narcissist may then distance the target from friends and family, either by manipulating loyalties or by filling every moment with turmoil, leaving little room for anyone else. Claiming to share special status with the target is also a common tactic, which both ties the narcissist and his or her prey together and distances the target even further.

Narcissists can groom best when the target is vulnerable to their tactics. A person who is already emotionally codependent is an ideal candidate for grooming, because codependents seek the support of others to shore up their challenged emotional stability. Narcissists exploit the codependent's need for support with multitactic, guilt-inducing manipulation that leaves the target feeling responsible for gaps in the relationship and any other real or imagined offenses that may well be concocted by the narcissist.

Narcissists, in fact, prowl for targets who may be in vulnerable circumstances: a person in financial trouble, someone who recently suffered the loss of a loved one, or a person who just went through a rough breakup. Narcissists aspire to be the "knight in shining armor" rescuing their "damsel in distress," and then, of course, holding their good deeds over the target's head for the rest of eternity.

Narcissists also use a desire we all have—to be loved and feel special—to manipulate the target into compliance by giving and taking away love and attention. The narcissist will tell the target he or she is special and unique, that the narcissist has never met anyone so wonderful. In the next instant, the narcissist may claim to despise the target and to never have loved him or her in the first place. Just as quickly, the first behavior may return.

Narcissists often respond to disappointment with vitriolic tirades, which can induce shock in the target, just as some creatures in nature, such as jellyfish, sting their prey before pouncing. Experiencing this ongoing hot-and-cold behavior, especially given the importance of the narcissist's love to the target, leaves the target exhausted, debilitated, and compliant.

What can be done about grooming? The first step in combating grooming behavior is to see through it and recognize it as manipulation. Rather than arguing with the narcissist—a battle that cannot be won—the target can refuse to participate, leaving the narcissist alone in the conversation. The best response, however, is to leave the relationship, to distance yourself from the narcissist, removing him or her from your life. Recognizing and breaking free from a narcissistic relationship may require the help of an experienced therapist. We will discuss more about leaving the narcissist in the following chapters.

3. LOVE BOMBING

In love bombing, the narcissist targets his or her prey with affection and the appearance of love. It is a grooming tactic that induces trust of, and even love for, the narcissist. Finding love is challenging enough without having to separate real love from the attentions of a manipulative impostor. A love bombing episode is simultaneously emotionally draining, confusing, and alluring. Lauren L'Amie's 2019 article in *Cosmopolitan* entitled "Are You Being Love Bombed?" defines love bombing as "the practice of showering a person with excessive affection and attention in order to gain control or significantly influence their behavior. The love bomber's attention might feel good, but the motive is all about manipulation. What separates love bombing from just regular honeymoon feelings is an abrupt switch—one moment they may be totally idealizing their partner, and the next, they'll cut them down to size in an effort to control them."

Part of the love bombing phase is idealization. This, by definition, is "regarding or representing something as perfect or better than in reality." During idealization with a narcissist, an individual is groomed—via love bombing, hoovering, and future faking—to be a source of supply, as the narcissist paints a convincing picture that the individual is perfect for the narcissist. The target is convinced that he or she is the soulmate that both of you have been waiting for all your lives—one in a million. During this time, trust and programming are instilled in the individual so that the person's suspicions and boundaries are reduced or removed entirely, and the narcissist can pounce.

Although the love bombing narcissist may change tactics once you are in his or her grasp, that switch, in and of itself, is not what separates the love bomber from a person who genuinely loves you. On a deeper level, the difference is motive. The narcissist employs love bombing not to love another person, but to lure that person into believing they are loved, so that they will become vulnerable to the rest of the narcissist's array of tactics and strategies, all of which will serve to satisfy the narcissist's sickness—his or her narcissistic personality disorder. Love bombing is an act in service to the narcissist's pathology. The narcissist is forever unsatisfied without a captive, and even with a captive may never know true satisfaction, which may be beyond his or her ability or scope of feeling.

Love bombing is at the forefront of the narcissist's stealth technology. Being well loved is one of life's great pleasures, and the narcissist is expert at giving the appearance of loving his or her target very, very well. Narcissists are expert actors, holding on to a relationship, keeping a person both physically and emotionally close with love as bait.

This lulls the target, keeping them willing to join or remain in the relationship. Who is more willing to participate in the give-and-take of a relationship than someone who feels loved? We are most apt to succeed in life when we have support systems, and the narcissist creates sham support systems that appear very real indeed.

4. GASLIGHTING

Gaslighting is mind control to make victims doubt their reality, according to Tracy Malone, founder of Narcissist Abuse Support (narcissistabusesupport.com). The term "gaslighting" is derived from Patrick Hamilton's 1938 play *Gas Light* and its 1940 and 1944 film adaptations, in which a woman named Paula is psychologically manipulated by her husband, Gregory, who makes small changes in her environment so as to convince her and others that she is insane.

At one point, he gives her an expensive family heirloom (a brooch) and then secretly removes it from her purse so that she believes she has lost it. Frequently, he removes one or more items from the living room and accuses her of misplacing them. He discourages a caring neighbor who wants to visit Paula, and he isolates her from caring friends and family.

When she points out these inconsistencies, she is told she is wrong and is led to believe she is delusional. The name of the play is derived from the gas lamps used to light the house, which the husband manipulates while claiming that the lighting in the house has not changed, even when the light grows dim. The husband's goal is to scour the house and take possession of his wife's inherited jewelry and money and, collaterally, to have her committed, leaving him in possession of all the wealth. In the movie, it is revealed that Gregory is a serial con artist who carefully planned this caper well in advance. He has absolutely no genuine feelings for Paula, whom he courted at a vulnerable moment of loss in her life. The movie, as well as the original script, very accurately portray the inner selfish workings and outwardly devious tactics of a narcissist. The movie has a very satisfying ending in which Paula has a moment of justice. We will not spoil it for you.

Gaslighting is a covert form of emotional abuse, instilling confusion and cognitive dissonance in the unsuspecting target as the abuser makes small changes—either physical or emotional—in the target's environment. The narcissist denies the changes and encourages the target's confusion, leading to his or her emotional instability and greater dependence on the narcissist. The tactic is akin to a poisonous spider or snake whose venom weakens its target, rendering it helpless. People who have experienced gaslighting describe it as crazy-making, head-spinning, or maddening. It's completely disorienting and very difficult to describe to others, leading to deep feelings of frustration.

5. FUTURE FAKING

Future faking occurs when a narcissist paints a false picture of the future intended to lull the supply, or target, into easy compliance. Narcissists are vicious and dangerous liars, using their creative skills to feed their targets a specifically designed portrait of a future they would love, if it ever existed, with the goal of making the individual willing to engage with the narcissist, so as to make the portrait real.

Future faking is a form of seduction. Narcissists are rarely adept at, or willing to participate in, the give-and-take required for deep inter-action and genuine relationships. Future faking is a substitute for human give-and-take; it effortlessly drives the narcissist's supply down a prosaic road of beautiful scenery, at the end of which the narcissist lies in wait. According to a blog post by Elijah Akin, "What Is Future Faking and Why Do Narcissists Do It?", narcissists pay little attention to the relationship as such. They are laser-focused on their goal of domination. If you worry about finances, the narcissist will talk about an anticipated huge inheritance. If you are insecure about finding a new house, the narcissist will talk about a house his family owns that will "someday" be his own. The promises, always occurring in the future, will somehow connect with your own ambitions and wishes. But it will be an eternally dangling carrot; nothing will ever actually materialize.

6. ISOLATION

Narcissists are adept at isolating their targets from others and any flow of real information that might puncture the illusion the narcissist creates. Employing isolation as a tactic has the twin benefits of removing potential support or help from the subject's reach and removing threats from the narcissist's vicinity, thereby shielding the narcissist.

Narcissists often employ divide-and-conquer skills, including ridicule, threats, and blame, to instigate conflict between family members and associates, isolating them from one another. Cognitive dissonance, the disconnect between one's feelings and perceived reality, can even isolate the target or others in the narcissist's sphere of influence from their beliefs about themselves. Narcissistic relationships are often so confusing that those who are in them find themselves isolated because the reality of the experience is so far removed from the norm and from what is painted by the narcissist as a successful relationship. The supply may fear being perceived by others as crazy for questioning or even describing the actions of the narcissist. Indeed, according

to a blog post on The Narcissist Family Files titled "4 Insidious Ways Narcissistic Abuse Isolates the Victim," friends and family may find the subject's claims to be far-fetched and hard to believe, thereby engendering further isolation. The target can't explain what is going on because the events are crazy and illogical in and of themselves. The experience of narcissistic abuse is often described as being similar to a nightmare in which you are trying to scream out but cannot.

Along with efforts to isolate the target, narcissists who coparent attempt to alienate the ex-spouse by making them appear incapable of proper parenting or "bad," "crazy," or "too strict." Sadly, the narcissist often gets away with this, duping attorneys, judges, social workers, and the legal system as a whole. Enlightening the legal system to the ways of the narcissist should be a top priority for society.

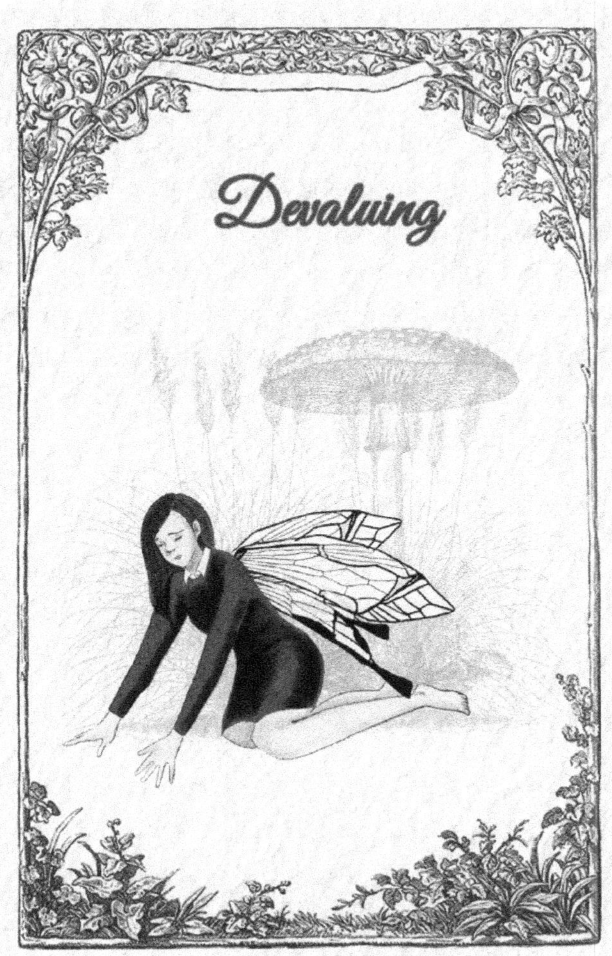

7. DEVALUING

Narcissists are experts at manipulating the perceptions of those around them. One effective way to dispel the veracity of a threatening claim or idea, or to weaken the arguments of the narcissist's supply, is via devaluing. The power of any idea or the person holding that idea is diminished through ridicule or a dismissive attitude. This can be extremely effective, given the narcissist's ability to lie credibly. If the character of the individual holding the ideas or opinions in question is demeaned, his or her opinions are apt to lose value with the narcissist's audience.

Devaluing is part of the narcissist's cycle of abuse. After idealization (praising, love bombing, future faking), the pendulum swings the other way; the narcissist begins to put the partner down or holds back on being intimate or showing affection. When the partner pushes back, the narcissist often turns things around—presenting himself or herself as the victim and blaming the partner, which further devalues the partner.

8. STONEWALLING

Narcissists use stonewalling, also known as the cold shoulder or silent treatment, either to punish those who dare to oppose them or to confuse their supply. When someone stops speaking to us, we tend to look for a reason that makes sense. Narcissists rarely make sense outside of their own twisted worlds. The narcissist may have little reason to stonewall beyond lashing out or sowing enough confusion to allow his or her other tactics to be more effective. Stonewalling is also a power play, because typically the target is the kind of person who likes to "talk it out" and settle things with open communication.

The silent treatment is anything but passive. It's directly aggressive and punishing. Once the person on the receiving end of the silent treatment behaves or believes as the narcissist wishes, normal communication may, or may not, resume. Expecting commonsense behavior from a narcissist is not realistic; the narcissist does not behave in a logical manner, but rather as a sick person who is acting out a pathology. The tension that flows from stonewalling may be viewed by the narcissist as a net positive, because it gives the narcissist control over communication and the relationship. It is also possible that the narcissist is reacting to diminished or withheld supply.

Being on the receiving end of silent treatment encourages an acceptance of responsibility by non-narcissists, or at least an examination of one's own behavior to find one's responsibility for the communication breakdown. When dealing with a narcissist, there may be no responsibility on the part of anyone but the narcissist, who is using the tactic as a means to dominate the supply. The most effective response to stonewalling is refusing to play along, according to an article on the Mindset Therapy website. Narcissists are strengthened by conflict and attention. When starved of these, their power is diminished.

Stonewalling, of course, is not the same as purposely taking a break in the discussion to let both participants cool down. You will never hear a narcissist say, "Listen, we're both hotheaded right now. Why don't we take an hour or so to calm down and then discuss this again when we are both a bit more rational." That would be a healthy communication technique. With a narcissist, it simply will not happen that way. He or she will slam a door or stop talking or just disappear. In a subtler style of stonewalling, narcissists may use a preferred mode of communication, texting for example, so that they may further control or limit the flow of information. If you have ever had an argument with a narcissist by text, you have experienced a particular kind of hell on earth.

9. FALSE CONSENSUS

Narcissists want us to believe that many others agree with their views, usually regarding demeaning opinions and discrediting of the target. Often this is used to convince the narcissist's target to capitulate and behave as the narcissist wishes. The formula can sound like this: "Of course you should take a day off for my birthday. Everyone I spoke to agrees with me. Even your friends." Or even more damaging: "None of your friends like you. They all think you're a wimp." Or the more undermining: "Who would put up with a person like you?" All very demeaning and a bit hard to identify, at first. Narcissists use false consensus to convince their supply to agree with ideas that are beneficial to the narcissist, by pointing out that other very reasonable, intelligent people share these ideas.

10. TRAUMA BONDS

A trauma bond occurs when a traumatized individual comes to trust whoever is causing the trauma. It is similar to Stockholm syndrome, which refers to captives who bond with their captors over time. It's purely a survival mechanism to deal with an untenable, traumatic circumstance. According to Sherry Gaba's post "Trauma Bonding, Codependency, and Narcissistic Abuse" on the *Psychology Today* website, the narcissist will exploit any codependent tendencies in the supply using love bombing or future faking, leading to a bond that is built on lies and vulnerability, which will then be exploited as the individual is controlled.

Whatever tactics are used, the feeling of love and connection the target experiences early on in the relationship may devolve into emotional, even physical, abuse, which may be tolerated given the trauma bond. Codependent individuals in a relationship with a narcissist tend to blame themselves for the abuse and look to the narcissist for

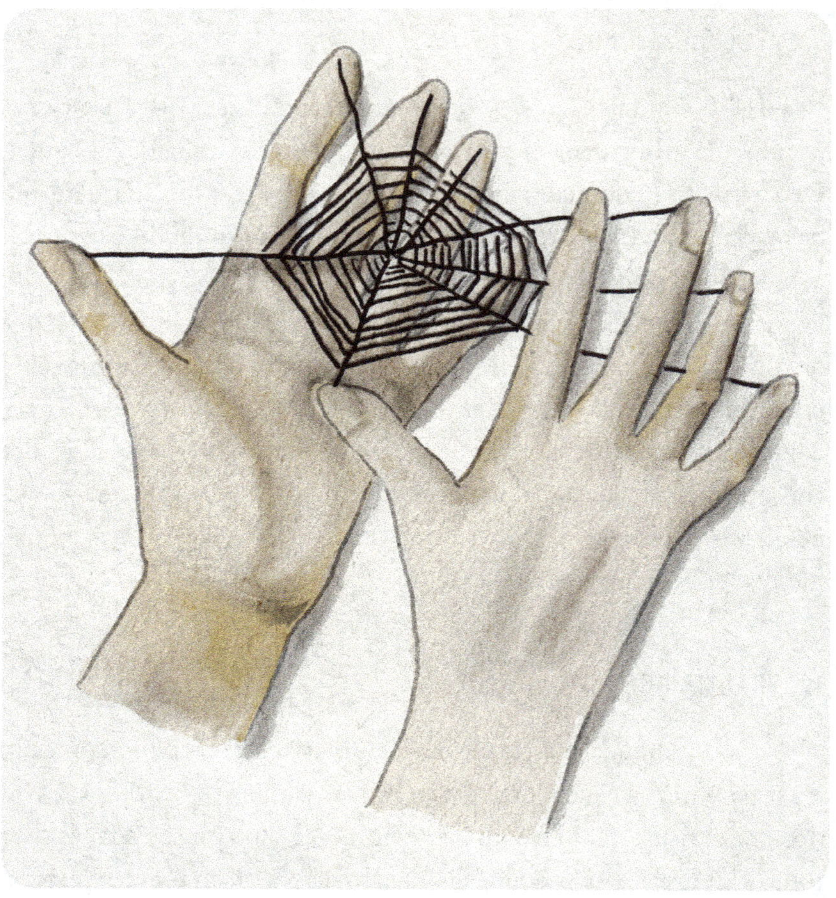

solutions. Trauma bonds lead to an acceptance of the status quo. If the supply attempts to leave or change the relationship, the narcissist has only to return to his or her original love bombing and/or future faking tactics to corral the target into complacency and obedience. Once the abuse is accepted, that acceptance becomes the norm, and an escalation of or return to abuse can occur and be accepted as well.

There are some very scientific explanations that add to our understanding of the trauma bond phenomenon. We become psychologically and neurochemically addicted to the narcissist. They tend to go to extremes. They have exciting "bucket lists," crave high-adrenaline adventure, and aspire to grandiose ideas like "soulmates," "perfect love," and once-in-a-lifetime experiences. They push our limits of tolerance. All this excitement, in addition to the negative and disturbing emotions narcissists are prone to cause, leads to the brain releasing endorphins and stimulants that are addictive. Even the narcissist's anger, aggression, and threats have the effect of producing a chemical fight-or-flight response that releases adrenaline. When we are away from the ever-provoking behaviors of the narcissist, we tend to feel as if everything is silent. We are not accustomed to the silence. Time spent in this tranquility can feel like a kind of withdrawal. People who leave narcissists often report that they are initially uncomfortable with the calm silence. But soon after they leave, they come to cherish it.

Behaviorally, narcissists establish an "intermittent schedule of reinforcement" in which they give love and affection unpredictably. Today might include a romantic, carefully prepared dinner, and tomorrow the narcissist can be abusive, demanding, and have you walking on eggshells. Such up-and-down behavior makes every moment unpredictable, but you know that it is possible to get that satisfying attention, so you keep trying to do so. The inconsistency is also addictive. Thousands of psychology experiments have demonstrated that we are more motivated by intermittent reinforcement than we are by constant rewards.

Physical and emotional separation from the narcissist, along with therapy with a trusted, experienced professional, are the recommended antidotes for the trauma bond. The supply must learn to see the narcissist's tactics for what they are, as well as to explore personal vulnerabilities that may have contributed to the narcissistic relationship.

11. FLYING MONKEYS

Flying monkeys are the narcissist's henchmen. Just as the Wicked Witch sent her flying monkeys after Dorothy and her companions in *The Wonderful Wizard of Oz*, narcissists co-opt others to aid in their efforts to subjugate and maintain sway over their supply. These assistants may themselves be narcissists or people suffering from any number of dysfunctions or disorders, including codependency or generalized anxiety disorder, who derive satisfaction or benefit from serving the narcissist. Flying monkeys may be every bit as devious and vicious as the narcissist, according to an article on PsychCentral

(psychcentral.com), and may employ the same arsenal of tactics and nefarious skills. Fending off the controlling behavior of one individual is challenging enough, but faced with a team or a small army, the individual can be demoralized, exhausted, and, eventually, compliant. The flying monkeys may or may not be aware of their role. They may have no idea that the narcissist, who could be a friend or relative, is anything but truthful. The flying monkeys may be members of your own family. The narcissist operates skillfully, deviously, and the realization that loved ones and friends are operating as a unified entourage can be quite disorienting.

Narcissists establish their monkeys using their professional skills to whisper secrets, sow the seeds of mistrust, tell stories with a minuscule kernel of truth, outright lie, play the victim, and conjure up every past transgression, whether real, imagined, or insignificant. The narcissist has definitely been talking behind your back. The skill at motivating these monkeys is quite amazing. Do not underestimate this ability.

In *The Wonderful Wizard of Oz* the winged monkeys are enslaved by the Wicked Witch and are controlled by a golden cap. Eventually, the brave Dorothy kills the Witch with water, obtains the golden cap, and frees the winged monkeys. Don't count on your narcissist's flying monkeys ever coming to their senses, though. The narcissist may never set them free.

12. SMEAR CAMPAIGN

When you finally confront, disagree with, or leave the narcissist, he or she will inevitably go into "narcissistic rage" and begin an all-out smear campaign. After all, what kind of person would have the audacity to leave someone as great as him or her? A terrible person! The narcissist will do anything and everything, regardless of consequences, to make you look like the bad one. Narcissists will use their flying monkeys, social media, attorneys, police, and, most disturbingly, their own children and family. They will lie, embellish, defame, and play the victim. In a smear campaign, the narcissist will do all this:

1. Search for a new supply and line up your replacement in advance.
2. Record you without permission and post it on Facebook.
3. Portray themselves as loving, devoted, and an innocent victim.
4. Write letters or emails to your boss or coworkers.
5. Call the police if you so much as raise your voice during a conflict.
6. Provoke you relentlessly, then call you crazy when you finally react.
7. Meet with your parents, relatives, and friends behind your back.
8. Discard you without notice, flaunt their new supply, then use your reaction to this as "evidence" that you were to blame for the problems in the relationship.
9. Use social media to draw you out and provoke you.
10. Contact previous romantic partners to obtain even more "dirt."

You will survive the flying monkeys and the smear campaign. It will weed out the real friends from the phonies. It will sometimes backfire with family members. Here are a few survival pointers:

1. Do not engage or attack the attacker. You have nothing to prove.
2. Do not contact or confront anyone who believes the smear.
3. Detach emotionally. Only share with trusted friends and family.

4. Limit use of social media: block, unfriend, and/or unsubscribe from the narcissist.
5. Cut all ties with people who are not supportive. Don't try to win them back.
6. Reflect on who you are; focus on strengths, abilities, self-esteem, and worth.
7. Trust that the truth will prevail over time. It usually does.

13. HOOVERING

Hoovering is when the narcissist offers manipulative, enticing texts, emails, phone calls, or direct statements meant to draw the target into their fold yet again. Hoovering is often used to draw a former supply back into the toxic relationship. It is a form of love bombing, albeit after the fact.

The narcissist might use nostalgia or references he or she knows are valued by the target to elicit the desired response, especially renewed attention and devotion. The narcissist may wait for a death in the family or the anniversary of some personal event to begin contacting you. Below are some examples:

"I'm watching our movie, thinking of us."

"Do you still have that red shirt I used to wear?"

"I dreamt about you."

"Just sayin' hi."

"Can we talk, just for one minute?"

"Congratulations on the promotion."

The narcissist may even seem apologetic or surprisingly benign and/or friendly in order to manipulate you back into their world. To

determine whether a person is hoovering, consider whether the narcissist is willing to change the focus or subject of the conversation. Narcissists tend to continue the tactic until their goal is achieved. Consider the timing of the connection. If it's on your birthday, former anniversary, or other date of importance in the former relationship, the goal may be to renew that relationship rather than to offer genuine support or well-wishes. The narcissist may lie about subjects of importance as a means of manipulation, knowing that the target will be emotionally moved and possibly apt to behave as the narcissist wishes. As the quip goes: "How can you tell when a narcissist is lying? Their lips are moving."

Spreading false gossip, pretending the relationship never ended, and threatening self-harm are all potential hoovering maneuvers. The narcissist is seeking attention and conflict. Refusing to address the fabrications is the only effective means of negating these antics.

14. FALSE SELF AND MASKS

Narcissists project themselves as the center of their universe. They project an appearance of being wonderful, physically attractive, sexy, charming, brilliant—impossibly perfect. They act as though they are precisely what their target needs. They project themselves as paragons of confidence, yet in truth, they are anything but. The narcissist's projected traits are a false self masking a deeply dysfunctional personality that desperately requires the attention and adoration of others to enable the narcissist to maintain his or her false self-image. Narcissists have such voracious appetites for attention because they lack self-esteem and self-worth, and often their self-loathing is just as great as these appetites.

The mask of a narcissist is very supple; it stretches based on the situation. Narcissists are on their best behavior in public and act the vilest at home. When they are wearing the mask, they appear to others as "such a nice person" or "a great guy!" The mask is like an insurance policy to protect them from the target's friends and family knowing the truth. Others will be shocked when they're informed that the narcissist has been abusing someone for years. The target will have to convince everyone that he or she is not the crazy one.

15. REPLACEMENT

Those who are in the clutches of the narcissist are their supply: their source of self-worth and self-esteem, their supply of power and control. If you are with a narcissist and you eliminate the narcissist's source of self, you are ripe for being discarded and replaced by someone more vulnerable to his or her weapons, someone more apt to shine the light of attention on the narcissist. More than likely, the narcissist has already begun the search, or even snared the next supply. They are so desperate that they will overlap supplies. In common language: they will cheat on you. Frequently.

To the narcissist, the supply is not a human being with dignity and feelings; he or she is a tool to be exploited, an object that can be replaced.

Since narcissists are expert at convincing their targets to see their false selves, they are admired by their targets, who see them as the light of their lives they project themselves to be. The target is convinced that the narcissist is a wonderful human being and a perfect partner—the only partner. Being discarded by the narcissist is being abandoned by this light of our life, whom we admire and adore. Being discarded by the narcissist is being deprived of our soulmate. Being discarded by a narcissist is agony. His or her love may have been completely manipulative and contrived, but our love was quite real. The overwhelming feeling of being discarded is profound loss.

16. OBJECT CONSTANCY

Individuals with narcissistic personality disorder lack object constancy. When disappointed by a family member, friend, or other person with whom they have a positive relationship, they lose their connection to the positive experiences that formed the foundation of the relationship and lapse into negative, often hurtful behavior, as a reaction to what they now perceive to be a negative relationship. This black-and-white, all-or-nothing, love-hate relationship is also the cornerstone of borderline personality disorder.

17. PARENTIFICATION

Parentification occurs when a narcissistic parent reverses roles in the parent-child relationship and burdens a child with an expectation of parental support and responsibility, expecting the child to meet the narcissist's needs as caregiver, confidant, financial supporter, and even sex object. Parentification can occur in more benign situations, such as in recently immigrated families where the parents have difficulty with English but the children are fluent in the language. The children fill out medical forms, answer mail, interpret documents, and sometimes even pay bills for the family. This level of access and authority within the family imposes an unnatural level of responsibility on the child. In the case of narcissists, they will expect an incredible amount of attention and sympathy when they are in need—for example, when they are feeling sick—but when the *child* isn't well, they will tell him or her to "grow up and stop whining." The narcissist expects the child to be a nurturing parent to fulfill defects within them but will never reciprocate such empathy or care.

18. TRIANGULATION AND SPLITTING

Triangulation occurs when the narcissist ensures that the flow of information between two groups flows through the narcissist, allowing the communication to be altered or warped to meet the narcissist's needs. Triangulation is closely related to "splitting," in which the narcissist turns one member of the triangle against the other by spreading rumors, telling lies about character, or just "making shit up." These disparaging comments, rumors, and accusations are very difficult to "undo." They have been repeated, reinforced, amplified, and sprinkled with just enough plausible fact to appear legitimate. All this is done behind your back. It's remarkable how much free time the narcissist seems to have!

19. THE NARCISSIST'S FAMILY SYSTEM

In families controlled by a narcissistic parent, children are often assigned roles that meet the narcissist's needs. These roles reflect the narcissist's view of the child as a one-dimensional source of supply, rather than as a person. These roles may include the following:

The Golden Child

This child is idealized as the perfect child who can do no wrong. Often, this child may be held up to the others as an example of desired behavior, speech, or appearance. Other children may be told, "Why can't you be as smart as they are?" or "Your older sister would never disgrace this family like you have!" The golden child, of course, is under a unique kind of pressure. He or she is the role model, the example of perfection, the "gold standard" of the family.

The Scapegoat

Essentially the polar opposite of the golden child, the scapegoat is blamed for problems in the family and is devalued for lacking attributes the narcissistic parent claims to value. The scapegoat may be the target of any number of narcissistic behaviors, including stonewalling, isolation, or gaslighting. The narcissist may accuse the scapegoat of being the cause of every problem or malady that befalls the other family members: "If it wasn't for you, we would not have had all this terrible luck." Or, more heinously, "It's your medical issues that have prevented this family from moving ahead," or "You can't be seen in public wearing those thick glasses."

Other family roles in a narcissistic household include the "lost child," the "mascot," and the "hero-caretaker." If you've been cast in one of these roles, you have already experienced how artificial and damaging it can be.

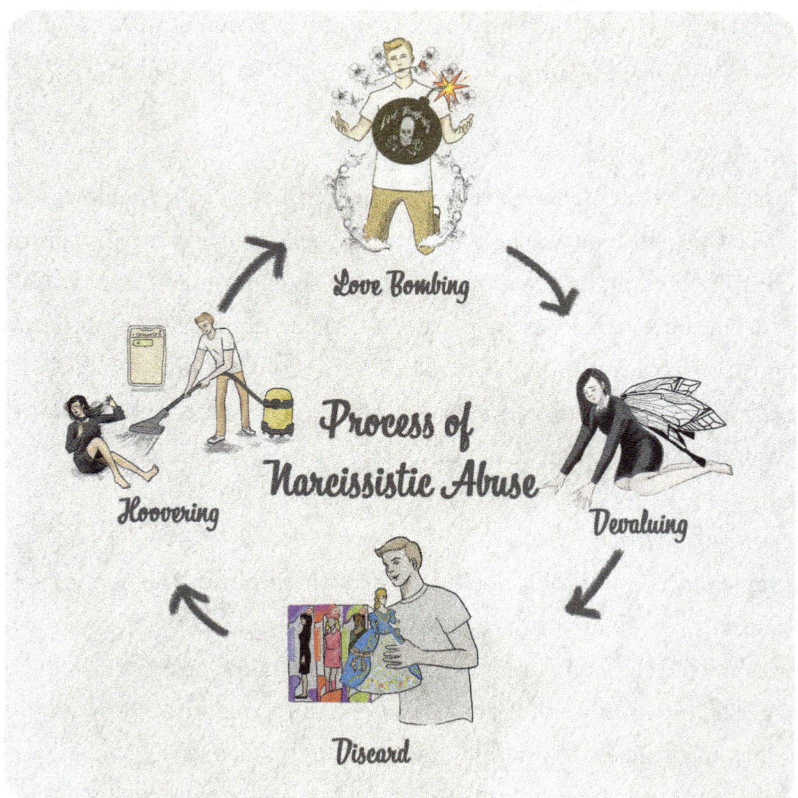

20. THE CYCLE OF ABUSE

Narcissists typically follow a cycle in their relationships that reflects the shallow, transitory nature of their needs. The cycle very effectively keeps the target hooked, addicted, and stuck, often eagerly waiting for the "good period" to return. The circular, repeating pattern of abuse may include any or all of the tactics previously described. Here's how this "wince and repeat" whirlwind unfolds:

Phase One:
Grooming, idealization, and love bombing are tactics used by narcissists to draw their targets into the web of deceit and to position them

as the ongoing supply. The targets are lulled into believing the narcissist admires and loves them, making them vulnerable to the narcissist's behavior. This stage is full of superlatives: "This is the best relationship I have ever been in." "We are soulmates, twin flames, bound by fate." "This was meant to be. It's a blessing from God, we are exactly alike."

In most cases, the narcissist has carefully stalked you, done a full background check on social media, and specifically targeted you like a criminal looking for the right house to burglarize. He or she may have groomed you for weeks, or even years, by systematically giving compliments, getting to know your personal likes, dislikes, and needs, and then exploiting all of them. The narcissist probably has two or three targets in mind at the same time. You are just the one who was receptive, hopeful, dedicated, kind, and generous. The perfect supply.

Love bombing is an overwhelming display of romantic gestures, love notes, cards, flowers, and promises. The narcissist flashes images of a fantastic future together and dangles golden carrots of riches, success, and eternal love in front of the supply to entice him or her. There will be exciting bucket-list adventures, tattoos with your name emblazoned on their body, grandiose plans, and great sex. It's intoxicating.

Phase Two:

Devaluing: when the narcissist is displeased with you or an aspect of your behavior, he or she will ridicule, demean, and devalue you, confusing you and causing you to question your behavior and, the narcissist hopes, conform it to the preference of the narcissist. This is the "yo-yo" phase. You know it's possible to feel loved and cared for, so what happened? The ups and downs of this phase can, and will, drive you crazy. It's exactly like living with Dr. Jekyll and Mr. Hyde. In behaviorist terms, this creates a very strong attachment because it is an "intermittent schedule of reinforcement." In other words, sometimes all your efforts pay off with a return of affection, sometimes nothing happens, and sometimes your efforts are met with arrogance, animosity, or aggression. It's the "sometimes" that is crazy-making.

Phase Three:

Discarding: when the narcissist believes he or she can no longer receive the narcissistic supply required from you, or when a better supply is found, he or she will discard you and move on to the next. This will be done in the most hurtful, obnoxious, toxic, demeaning, and damaging way possible. Don't expect anything like, "Listen. I don't think this marriage is working out. We've tried, and I just don't think we're getting along. Let's part amicably for the sake of the children and make this breakup as easy as possible for both of us." That's for normal, unsuccessful relationships. Your breakup with a narcissist will be a shitstorm.

Phase Four:

Hoovering: But wait! There's more! You'll be sitting at your computer weeks, months, or even years after your breakup, beginning the arduous recovery process, finally getting back on your feet emotionally, when you'll get an email or text message. It'll be from an account you don't immediately recognize, and it will read something like this: "Dreamt about you last night." "Remember that week in Aruba?" "I'm very sick." Or just "Hi." It's the narcissist. Just like the famous, reliable vacuum cleaner brand of the same name, the narcissist is "hoovering," trying to suck you in, attempting to pull you back into the circle of chaos.

A thousand thoughts and feelings will be triggered, because the contact reignites, for an instant, associations of love bombing, romance, and the exciting aspects of the relationship. You may feel that you miss them. Or hate them. Or are enraged by the contact. But feelings will certainly be triggered. Technically, the dopamine receptors in your brain will reignite along previously dug-in paths. A tinge of addiction will reemerge.

You have to admit it: it may be difficult to resist contact again. But it is one hundred percent certain that if you fall for it and respond, the narcissist will pull you into the circle only to devastate and discard you again. He or she has not "gotten better," has not changed, is the same pathological narcissist that hurt you in the first place. Maybe he or she has developed even more disgusting, evil ways. Do not respond in any way. Block the person in every way possible.

One more aspect of the cycle of abuse: the cycle spins faster and faster and grows shorter and shorter over time. The great times will be short-lived and impossible to maintain, and the abuse will become more rapid-fire. The sooner you get off the merry-go-round, the better.

21. NARCISSISTIC INJURY

Narcissistic injury is an early life trauma or lack suffered by the narcissist that interfered with normal emotional growth and the development of self-worth, contributing to the narcissist's pathology. Narcissistic injury is caused by a lack of compassionate parenting, an absent sense of safety, physical or mental abuse, or parental rejection. Don't feel too sorry for the narcissist just yet. Some recent research suggests that narcissism is simply inborn, genetic, or neurochemical in nature and not necessarily a result of adverse childhood experiences.

22. NARCISSISTIC RAGE

When a narcissist is devalued or defied in some way—shamed, ignored, or insulted—he or she will often fly into a rage that far exceeds what circumstances would appear to warrant. This dysregulated behavior is a certainty in a narcissistic relationship because narcissists perpetually seem to feel insulted in some way. Acts of defiance against the narcissist trigger a connection to the narcissistic injury, discussed above.

23. COGNITIVE DISSONANCE

Cognitive dissonance has a profound effect on the targets of narcissistic abuse. They often find that their experiences, as controlled by the narcissist, do not match their feelings or perceptions. The bewildering disconnect that is cognitive dissonance has also been referred to as being in "oppositeland," in that the target's experiences, especially with the narcissist, are the opposite of normal perceptions and notions of reality. It's very disorienting. We will discuss cognitive dissonance later in the book.

24. MYSTIFICATION

Mystification refers to the narcissist's abject denial of the target's feelings, thoughts, and ideas even in the face of hard evidence. If the narcissist's partner says, "I'm not feeling well," the narcissist will respond, "You're just fine!" If you express a feeling, the narcissist will say, "That's not the right way to feel." Since we tend to internalize words and ideas that are frequently repeated, we will tend to believe the contradictions if we're exposed to the narcissist long enough.

THE DISORIENTATION OF NARCISSISTIC ABUSE

Here are some examples from real cases of narcissistic abuse. You can identify the tactics being used by the narcissist in each case. When reading about these experiences, it is easy to feel fear, disorientation, and confusion.

Roberta was told by her new partner that "it was fate" that they were both from other countries. He added to this bond by pointing out their strong connection and great shared sexual experiences. As the relationship progressed, however, Roberta's partner began to criticize her constantly when out in public.

Before her experience with her narcissist, Claudia spent much of her free time with her girlfriends, was successful at work, was promoted, and had a good quality of life. Then she met her narcissist, who claimed to understand all the "pressures of success." He gradually began to occupy most of her free time, insisted on moving in with her, and eventually started to criticize most of her friends. One by one, Claudia's friends stopped inviting her to social events. She found herself isolated and couldn't quite understand how it all happened.

Harriet tried to reason with her narcissist. When she attempted to express her feelings, she was accused of being dramatic, fragile, and "exaggerating everything." He was expert at making her feel as if the manipulations she saw were all in her head. Harriet was someone who normally had a high level of self-confidence, was levelheaded, and was anything but crazy.

All her life, Jessica had to listen to her mother's critical comments about her physical appearance, focused especially on her hair and weight. When Jessica was preparing to attend her high school prom, her mother focused on "how pretty" Jessica's classmate was. Comments like these shook her confidence and kept her from confronting her mother.

Sheryl was bewildered by her narcissist's vicious cycle of behavior. She believed this behavior created a trauma bond that kept her in line. Any engagement at all would leave her drained. She did not feel like herself anymore. Her energy was very low, and she found herself to be uncharacteristically unmotivated at work.

Theresa was drawn to her narcissist when he shared with her that he was struggling with major childhood trauma. His apparent vulnerability hooked her into the relationship because she knew that she could help him and make a difference in his life. She felt good about being needed but over time realized that she never received any gratitude or appreciation from her partner.

After a trial separation, Rachel's ex, Sean, spread lies on Instagram that she was an abusive person and posted long narratives making himself out to be a victim. He constantly tried to make her feel bad. He told her that all the therapists she had seen had fed into her lies and insecurities. Rachel's daughter now resents her because Sean convinced her that Rachel favored and spent more money on a younger sibling. Rachel discovered numerous text conversations, of which she was unaware, between Sean and several of her friends.

STRANGE THINGS THAT ONLY A NARCISSIST WILL DO

1. Bask in attention for some insignificant accomplishment while calling your proud moments of achievement "childish bragging."
2. Wait until the last possible moment to bring up important information, such as saying, "I forgot to tell you your car has a flat tire," right before you leave for work.
3. Ruin every single holiday and celebration (except their own).
4. Value and admire a stranger's opinion above that of friends or family.
5. Be obsessed with their own appearance and take an astoundingly long time getting ready to go out.
6. Remain eerily stone-faced, or actually smirk, while you are crying.
7. Have an absolutely fantastic memory for anything negative you have ever done, no matter how long ago. Have sudden amnesia about things that have been completely resolved.
8. Remain "friends" with every ex they ever had.

QUESTION: Of all the techniques that a narcissist uses as a means of control, which did you find the most devastating?

DR. FRED

I was very susceptible to the silent treatment, stonewalling, and ghosting. I'm a talker and a communicator. My propensity is to solve issues, talk reasonably, and settle differences. It goes against every fiber of my being to avoid things and leave them unsettled. As you'll hear many times in this book, stonewalling is not the same as taking a break from a heated discussion and getting back to it when cooler thoughts prevail. Stonewalling is a type of abuse. It is deliberately refusing to engage in communication. My narcissist was absolutely, keenly aware that the silent treatment was basically my "Room 101." To quote George Orwell, "It's the worst thing in the world."

DR. ROBIN

Since I'm a generous and warm person, I found the pattern of covert withholding and punishment for purposes of control to be the most devastating. It was like constantly living in a chess match. The narcissist was like a spider; I never knew when he would jump out and do something that was creepy.

6

The Narcissist Effect

CONSEQUENCES OF BEING IN A RELATIONSHIP WITH A NARCISSIST

Experiencing a narcissistic relationship is like finding oneself in a horror movie that is both real and never-ending. Even for the most well-adjusted people, being on the receiving end of a steady stream of criticisms and attacks, interspersed with love bombing, future faking, and emotional manipulation, can lead to anxiety and challenged self-esteem. That's what this nefarious pathology can do when mixed with the target's love and a reluctance to leave the narcissistic relationship. There is nothing else like it, and it is very difficult to explain this to others.

Our failure to change or escape from the narcissist can lead to despair and depression. The future can look bleak when we feel trapped by the narcissist in our lives, even when we become aware of what is going on. That's why seeking professional help from a therapist experienced in working with people who have been in narcissistic relationships is essential. Seeing through the manipulation and being supported through the difficult separation process can make all the difference when it comes to the effectiveness of therapy.

People with once-healthy social skills may develop social anxiety because their experience with the narcissist has ruined their confidence. Shaming and devaluing can keep a person "in line" and can poison relationships when performed in front of others.

A once-cheerful person who is now perpetually on edge, waiting for the next "shoe to drop," may become easily agitated or irritated. A trauma bond may lead the narcissist's partner to criticize others in a subconscious attempt to mimic the narcissist. The target of the narcissist may become self-destructive, seeking solace in alcohol or other drugs to ease his or her experience. When no other escape seems possible and when no understanding friends or family seem to be available, the target may buy too many things from Amazon, overindulge in video games, or go to other extremes. The truth may be that supportive people are, in fact, available, but the narcissist has created the illusion of isolation. The target might not realize that reaching out may help. Others may be supportive, but accepting genuine concern from others will be challenging. Without support, a narcissist's target may be so desperate as to engage in self-harm, particularly if he or she is the child of a narcissistic parent and has had no healthy adult role model.

A person who is in a relationship with a narcissist may feel socially isolated, deserted by former friends and family, seemingly for no reason. As Zari Ballard points out in *When Evil Is a Pretty Face*, "No matter how smoothly it starts, a relationship that involves one partner having a narcissistic personality will inevitably take a mind-numbing turn for the worst, leaving the victim partner in emotional shreds, trying to make sense as to why it all happened."

Our minds rebel when faced with the narcissist's behavior. We do not want to believe that a formerly loving, seemingly supportive, stable partner could turn on us and carry out deceitful, premeditated attacks, using others who love us as weapons. We may be suddenly fearful, anxious, and mistrustful of others who have always been trustworthy. Narcissism is a pathology that affects all those who come in contact with it, potentially distorting their sense of reality, removing them from the ranks of the well-adjusted and often from contact with anyone at all.

Because the initial phase of the narcissistic relationship is so positive and so convincingly loving and wonderful, the partner may find rebounding from its loss difficult and painful. Feelings of guilt, encouraged by the narcissist, may be ongoing. The partner may obsess over the relationship, which seemed too good to be true. He or she may suffer from insomnia or nightmares, detachment or dissociation. Loneliness, anhedonia (inability to feel pleasure), and loss of interest

MINDSET of NARCISSIST

in once-pleasurable activities may also continue for a time, especially if help from a trained therapist is not quickly employed.

The responses of once well-adjusted people to the narcissist in their lives may be a part of the narcissist's supply. The narcissist creates confusion and seeks adoration, admiration, pacification, gratification, conciliation—all of which are reasonable responses to conflict. However, they are ineffective as means of ending the narcissist's attacks.

The following are some experiences common to people in narcissistic relationships, as compiled on Angie Atkinson's website Queenbeeing.com, along with our observations as practicing psychologists. Following these will be a list of clinical diagnoses that may also result from or be exacerbated by narcissistic relationships.

YOU WALK ON EGGSHELLS.

Narcissists are often volatile and may be triggered by any behavior they disapprove of or perceive as threatening in any given moment. Over time, this can lead the person in the narcissistic relationship to be reluctant to speak or act for fear of triggering an outburst. These outbursts can be traumatizing. They hurt!

You are confused by any conflict because it feels like your reality is being twisted (gaslighting).

Experiencing conflict with a narcissist can lead you to question your reality. You will be thrown off guard by references to events that never happened or happened differently than what you experienced, or by the narcissist denying facts that you have seen or heard. You will find yourself increasingly hiding your real feelings and staying quiet when it would be totally appropriate to speak up.

You are required to check in or touch base constantly, and it feels as if your every move is monitored. You are anxious if you do not check in, or if you happen to check in late.

Narcissists are extremely controlling and often expect anyone in their sphere of influence to adhere to their timetable. They often treat others like children, particularly when they are not receiving their supply of admiration and submission. You may feel belittled, disrespected, and patronized.

You feel sad when your partner jokes with you, because the jokes feel like hidden criticism or emotional attacks. This is especially true for those who normally enjoy joking as a way of communicating with others.

Emotionally mature humor is not hurtful, whereas sarcasm is anger hidden beneath a thin veneer of humor. A narcissist's attempts at "humor" at your expense are anything but funny; rather, they are painful efforts at coercion and control. When questioned, the narcissist might point to your usual sense of humor as evidence that the narcissist's humor ought to be appreciated.

YOU APOLOGIZE WHEN YOU HAVE DONE NOTHING WRONG.

Given the nearly constant confusion and pain caused by being in a relationship with a narcissist, the desire to stop their attacks with apologies is understandable. But narcissists are rarely mollified. Instead, apologies are perceived by narcissists as their due and as doorways to further abuse. Apologies are used as permission to continue the abusive behavior; they are held up as evidence of validation. You fear "hot and cold" moods, so you are trying all the time to keep the peace or fix things. You are hypervigilant over your partner's mood.

Narcissists are as unpredictable as rabid animals. A person in a relationship with a narcissist may be in a perpetual state of hyperawareness, hoping to avoid the nightmarish conflict that can occur at any time, independent of any apparent stimulus. Once conflict does ensue, the narcissist's target may frantically struggle to appease, fix, reconcile, pacify, or otherwise give the narcissist whatever is necessary to end the current tirade, which is exactly what the narcissist wants.

YOU FEEL AS IF YOUR PARTNER NEVER SEES THE GOOD IN YOU AND BELITTLES YOUR ACHIEVEMENTS.

It is possible that the narcissist is incapable of seeing the good in you. But that has nothing to do with you and everything to do with the narcissist, who is incapable of seeing the good in anyone but himself or herself. Your achievements are no less worthy because the narcissist does not recognize them. Narcissists see only their own achievements and those that serve their needs. Beyond that, they see only supply— that which feeds their voracious appetite for admiration, adoration, and validation. The narcissist will ignore, belittle, mock, and diminish your achievements.

YOU FEEL AS IF SEX IS AN OBLIGATION OR THAT IT HAPPENS AGAINST YOUR WILL. YOU ARE THREATENED WITH LEAVING IF YOU REFUSE.

For a narcissist, sex is not an expression of love, since the true narcissist is not capable of love. For them, sex is for their gratification. Sex is their due. The expectation of sex is an accoutrement to the narcissist's claim to power. Not only is sex not about love, it is not about you, but only about the narcissist. Do not expect gratification from sex with a narcissist. Sex is another weapon the narcissist uses to meet his or her needs. In the bedroom, the narcissist will mock and belittle your preferences and desires while being forceful regarding their own.

STRESS IN THE RELATIONSHIP CAUSES YOU TO SPACE OUT OR DISSOCIATE EASILY.

The constant conflict that is an essential component of the narcissist's supply is difficult to tolerate. Depending on the individual and his or her previous experiences, escape from this painful interaction may require any number of dissociative behaviors, including obsessive TV or movie watching, alcohol or drug abuse, or self-harm. Healthier behaviors include spending time with friends, exercising, yoga, or meditation, especially if these are part of a separation process with the oversight of a good therapist.

HOLIDAYS OR VACATIONS ARE STRESSFUL TO PLAN BECAUSE YOU FEAR YOUR PARTNER WILL SABOTAGE THE FUN.

Narcissists often possess powerfully magnetic personalities and can ensure that the love bombing and future faking effectively convince the partner of the pleasure of their company; yet their mercurial natures and their tantrums are difficult to tolerate. Planning a vacation with a narcissist is to live in the tension between these two extremes—at once drawn by the partner's charm and repelled by their volatile unpredictability. The narcissist in your life will find a way to ruin completely any plans, from the initial choice of where to go for your holiday, to the travel accommodations, to the hotel room, meals, activities, shopping, and interactions with other vacationers. You will be miserable, and they will make sure of it. The cognitive dissonance, the contradiction between how you are "supposed" to feel (while on a perfect beach in Aruba, for example) and how miserable and lost you actually feel, will be agonizing.

YOU CANNOT RATIONALLY DISCUSS ISSUES WITHIN THE RELATIONSHIP.

For the most part, mature partners in successful, healthy relationships are able to communicate about the relationship with clarity and without each participant causing the other pain. Narcissists do not qualify as mature partners, however. What passes for communication is often subtle (or not so subtle) verbal manipulation or abuse—words used for effect. The partner will find his or her insecurities used against them. Indeed, the partner may come to have new insecurities. Narcissists are experts at breaking down the well-adjusted individual and causing and exploiting vulnerability. Attempting to discuss the relationship with a narcissist is not safe, as the relationship itself is not safe.

Soothing and reassuring the abusive narcissist doesn't work—unless they want it to work. The impulse to return the relationship to "the way it used to be" is a fallacy, because the relationship never really *was* the way it used to be; it was a lure, a smokescreen to attract you as the narcissist's supply. Again, your feelings were quite genuine and heartfelt. Not theirs, though.

YOU MAY FIND YOURSELF CONSTANTLY COMPARED TO OTHERS AND FOUND WANTING.

When you bring up the narcissist's attacks, he or she may say you are too sensitive, no matter how awful the attacks were. The narcissist tells you that previous partners dealt with those situations far better than you do. The narcissist will point to others and ask why you cannot be more like them. Your looks and personality, your habits and speech are fodder for comparisons that leave you on the short end. The narcissist will not admit that these attacks are anything less than appropriate expressions of reasonable emotion or fact. The narcissist will belittle, ignore, or negate your feelings in an attempt to prove your inferiority to almost anyone else. The narcissist will induce jealousy as he or she showers others with affection and attention that were once reserved for you. Affection will be turned off and on strategically. It is as though your supply of air is cut off, then suddenly returned, only to be shut off again. Their actions leave you gasping. They make you feel as though you are the abuser and the narcissist is the victim. The narcissist accuses you of being unstable or crazy, and in your isolated, agitated state you do, in fact, feel that way.

If you feel as if you are addicted at this stage, it's because you are. Removing yourself from the forces of intermittent attention can be similar to cocaine withdrawal. There's a driving force compelling you to stay in this unhealthy relationship for the "good stuff" or to pine away based on visceral memories of the love bombing phase. Your brain craves the adrenaline, whether it was caused by excitement or misery.

YOUR FORMER SELF IS GONE.

The pain caused by your narcissist feels physical. You can no longer identify your boundaries. You have lost your sense of self. Like Echo, you have disappeared as a distinct entity and seem to exist only as a support for and reaction to the narcissist. Your ambitions and dreams no longer matter. They, like the person who had them, have been subsumed by the narcissist. You may not even recognize yourself in the mirror as a result of this depersonalization. It is extremely disturbing.

Before deciding to see a therapist, you may attempt to first reach out to a friend—only to find that the narcissist has gone to that person first and poisoned that person's perception of you, convincing them that you are the sick and twisted one gaslighting them. And, though well-intentioned, most friends and family will not fully understand what the mechanisms and effects of narcissistic abuse entail. Often, they will offer terrible or even dangerous advice and meaningless comfort: "Maybe the two of you should go to a marriage counselor"; "I can't believe John would do that—he's such a nice guy!"; "Every marriage goes through ups and downs. Things will get better in time." This is the harsh reality: it's almost impossible to comprehend the true menace that is narcissistic abuse.

In *When Evil Is a Pretty Face*, Zari Ballard explains that, in her opinion, the female narcissist "is a conniving, beguiling character that enjoys a level of evil that far exceeds that of her male counterpart." She will find and exploit vulnerabilities immediately and determine her "game plan" for the pathological relationship, then adhere to that agenda for as long as it satisfies her. Her demeanor is hypnotic, mesmerizing. Her sexual attention is perfectly crafted to suit her target's desires and sexual style. While it may be that female narcissists tend to exhibit different aspects of the pathology than their male counterparts, the male narcissist is not to be underestimated.

Narcissists of both sexes make us dizzy with changes in their personalities. They love us and always have. They hate us and always have. They are hurt by our abuse and betrayals, and they claim to be wounded by our attentions toward others, even though we have never turned our attention to others.

PSYCHOLOGICAL DISORDERS AS A RESULT OF NARCISSISTIC ABUSE

Narcissists' targets may suffer from C-PTSD—complex post-traumatic stress disorder. They may be tormented by emotional flashbacks that leave them feeling like overwhelmed, abandoned children. Once-secure individuals may be subject to immobilizing fear, shame, alienation, grief, depression, or rage. They may experience toxic shame and a plummeting sense of self-worth, despite being outwardly successful and secure. They may come to believe they are fatally flawed, ugly, or stupid.

Complex post-traumatic stress disorder is a common response to prolonged or intense trauma and may be experienced by anyone exposed to a narcissist. Clinically, we have seen these symptoms in short-term narcissistic relationships as well as in abusive marriages that have lasted decades. Narcissists can work very quickly in destroying your well-being. Symptoms of C-PTSD include the following:

Anxiety

Insomnia

Hypervigilance

Nightmares

Over-reactivity

Addictive behavior

Self-destructive thoughts or behavior

Intrusive thoughts

The narcissistic relationship may cause physical symptoms. You may have headaches or body aches. You may find that you are losing your hair, your skin integrity, or even your teeth! You may feel muscle tension, particularly when you're around your narcissistic partner. When your partner is happy or simply leaving you alone, your mind may flood with relief, and your endorphin, dopamine, and serotonin levels elevate.

We think we intuitively understand what makes a person good or evil; we believe we can recognize the difference, and then we find that everything we thought was true of our "loving" partner is false, and traits we would have labeled as evil were hidden behind an utterly convincing false front.

You treated your partner with compassion, and it was turned against you, wounding you, which your partner either denied or enjoyed. You struggle against the truth—that you have been in a relationship with an evil partner. You wonder how you, a discerning, mature adult, could have been so blind.

Once you determine to break away, you find yourself repeatedly pulled back into the swirling vortex, once again surrounded by lies that seem true and truths that seem false. If you are somehow able to remove yourself from the narcissistic relationship, perhaps with the help of a good therapist experienced in treating partners of narcissists, you may find yourself devastated by the loss of the relationship. Love bombing, future faking, and grooming in general lift the relationship to great heights in the partner's perception. The loss of the relationship means a fall from these apparent heights, with devastating effect when you slam into the apparent reality of the "ground." Numbness and shock follow. You are in withdrawal. Your spirit is deeply wounded. You feel as though you are ill, and in a very real sense, you are.

Regaining trust in others and recovering your own equilibrium may be difficult, may take time and hard work with a trained professional. Yet returning to yourself—an improved, more aware self—is very much within reach.

Descriptions of the effects narcissists have on their partners, family members, employees, and others tell only part of the story. The depths of acute pain and confusion felt by those in narcissistic relationships cannot be reduced to abstract description and are best communicated by the individuals themselves in their own words. These are from support groups we have facilitated, both in person and online.

Julie: "I am in this group because I have a narcissistic and borderline mother. I'm still trying to deal with that. I have a lifetime of her. There are a lot of other issues. Every time I think things have gotten better, she does something that is going to make me angry again. I'm still trying to work through that. She pushes my buttons to make me angry and to get me to do things. That's why I'm here."

Ruth: "I don't know what to say or do. When he does say these things, I get confused and feel as though I am losing my memory, while at the same time I seem to have my memory in other situations. The whole thing is just horrible."

Nancy: "My ex kicked down a door while I hid in a closet and called the police. I was terrified. The police came and they made me feel like I was the one that was crazy. He paints himself in a calm and put-together way, and makes me seem like I am always undone. I feel like I lost a part of myself—like he stole it!"

Jason: "I didn't feel like myself anymore. It's a hard thing to explain. I've felt like myself for as long as I can remember—at every age. Comfortable in my own skin. Yet here, I no longer felt like me. That's when I knew something was wrong."

Paula: "I am actually in the middle of a very, very difficult divorce. I was married for twenty-five years and in the relationship for thirty years. The two adult kids were with me. So, actually I did have a major milestone this week. It has actually been a very terrible two weeks. I thought I was almost dying two weeks ago. It's just really difficult. Then I got a lawyer, and I think this was a good move. To actually get some representation, and most importantly, I did send my last ever email to him this week and I feel really awesome about it. That was building up to a restraining order if he doesn't comply . . . Today I've been really angry for some reason, including wanting to throw all my clothes away in my closet. Everything that reminds me of him and my life with him. My therapist said it's okay to keep the things I really value, but it's very disturbing."

Carolyn: "I didn't understand his mood swings. They were scary, and it seemed that I caused them. He would say that whatever he was upset about was my fault. And I bought into that. I was empathetic toward him. He started alienating me from my friends and family. I couldn't work and he made me feel worthless about that. I believed him. I thought I loved him and I thought he loved me. That seemed like the truth."

Julie: "I started going to therapy, and I learned to put myself first. As soon as I started doing that, my boyfriend (the narcissist) began backing off."

Ruth: "I took some courses to enhance my career and I could just feel my mother telling me I would fail because I was a 'screwup.' Part of me still believed that, even all these years—decades—later. My therapist suggested I do affirmations, using my voice to combat my mother's. This has been helping."

Robert: "I've been out of the relationship for years, but because we have children together, the effects continue. She poisons our kids' views of me. I can't believe these trials and storms are still going on. The fact that it involves my children is awful. I've known and loved them since the day they were born, yet all of a sudden we feel like strangers."

Norma: "I joined a group recently because I was in not only one, but two narcissistic relationships. One—my partner had highly narcissistic traits, and the second one was a full-blown narcissistic relationship. I am still healing from it, although we have had no contact for a couple of months now. I am still healing from that trauma bond and my own codependency issues. I've been told that healing can take quite some time."

Vikki: "I realized recently that I was definitely cheated on. I was even cheated on prior to our marriage. It hurts to know that. I think I should be more confident going into my court session with my new lawyer, but I still feel uneasy. I sent my last email to him two weeks ago. I want no contact with him, so everything is going through lawyers. My anxiety has decreased as I started exercising, but I still feel anxious just at the thought of going there. It is very frustrating for me to be experiencing this anxiety because this is not who I am. I cannot recognize myself because I cannot control it."

Ann: "My ex narcissist boyfriend found my Instagram recently and tried contacting me. I went into a panic. It all came back! There was also a friend in my life that is a narcissist and I cut him off very quickly. I could not handle it because he wanted to date me, but I have a boyfriend. He got a new phone to contact me after I blocked him. He also tried contacting my boyfriend to break us up. This narcissistic friend who wanted to date me would send me food at work, take me out to dinner and persistently chase me, even when I declined."

Sharon: "I started going back to the gym and to church after a while of not going. Church was very comforting. It's going to take a while to get back to reality after your whole life was an illusion. My ex was of a different religion, and I felt like I left my whole self behind when I was with him. When I was in church, I felt like I could forgive him. I want to move forward toward a healthier life. The trauma bond kept me in the loop until I cut him off. I felt tied to him, and that I needed him. My views were so distorted. No contact seemed like a punishment at first, but it's a requirement for survival."

Karin: "It's been a bad week. A constant cycle of mind games, and he is desperately clinging to the marriage, telling me that the fact that we are having problems is all my fault. He says I've destroyed everything and I'm so selfish. The blame and guilt are tremendous. Well, now I've got a lawyer to defend me. Now the things he's said don't seem to matter as much. The lawyer is a buffer. And I guess time away from him does that. Yet now I feel guilty for still loving him and having sympathy for him. It's been going on for fifteen years, through our entire marriage. My oldest daughter told him he should leave. That she understands is a big help. That anyone understands is a big help."

Hannah: "I feel like I'm in a downward spiral and I don't want to get out of bed. I don't want to do anything. Seeing my therapist has been a great start because, even though I still feel this way, my therapist is giving me direction and some motivation. I had none of either before. I told my therapist I'm going to push through my feelings and do something to get past this. And I will."

Francis: "My therapist told me that I'm going to hear very similar stories when talking to other victims. He said I'm going to be comfortable pretty quickly in the group because so many narcissists seem to follow the same protocol. Like a textbook example—they are all the same. He said the similarities are almost scary."

It is best to admit that the narcissist has, in fact, had an effect on you. You are a different person for having interacted with a narcissist. You are now more aware of yourself, enlightened about how others may operate to manipulate you, and much stronger for the experience.

If you are not quite at this point yet, be patient. You will not regret leaving the narcissist.

ARE YOU THE NARCISSIST?

At some point in your ordeal with the narcissist, you will find yourself asking this question. We have all questioned our own mental health in the throes of abuse and devaluation. If you have to ask, though, then the answer is . . . no! Narcissists do not ponder their psychological well-being. They do not self-reflect. And they certainly are not troubled when thinking about the things they have done to hurt others. Only a mentally healthy person does this. You are not the narcissist.

ABOUT CLOSURE

Every human being seeks closure after a relationship does not work out. Individuals appreciate a nice, meaningful wrap-up, maybe even an adult discussion about why the relationship didn't thrive. They hope for some kind words about the good times, some mutual compliments, and some logical conclusions about what happened and why. Partners wish each other well and move on with dignity and respect. When dealing with a narcissist (to paraphrase Gru from *Despicable Me*), "In terms of closure . . . you'll have no closure!" Don't look for any, don't seek any, and don't expect any. Your closure will be internal: "I'm outta here. I learned what I could, improved myself, and won't let that ever happen again!"

In what ways did you feel different from your normal self while you were with the narcissist?

DR. FRED

Really, that was my turning point. I was not my "self." I had become someone I barely recognized. And I felt ashamed of myself for putting up with the abuse. I had been generally happy, enthusiastic, motivated, creative, outgoing, productive, and very high-energy. Somewhere in the narcissistic relationship, I had lost all this! I was depressed, quiet, unproductive, isolated, nervous, and sad. This was definitely not who I was. Something was very wrong. Eventually these feelings were simply not tolerable and led to action, and my path to recovery and freedom.

DR. ROBIN

I'm an outgoing, happy person who takes care of herself and loves to set goals and achieve them. When I was with the narcissist I was depressed, anxious, isolated, unproductive, and disorganized. When I finally left the narcissist and cut all contact, I couldn't believe the abundance of energy that had come back into me. Narcissists are known for sucking the energy of others, and, unfortunately, this worsens over time.

Freeing Yourself from the Narcissist

7

Bye-Bye, Narcissist!

STEP 1. UNDERSTANDING THE NARCISSIST

You are at the beginning of an amazing excursion! It's a journey away from the toxic, abusive narcissist and a trip back to yourself. If you have suffered with a narcissistic relationship, then you have been through hell. It's time to escape. In the next eight chapters, we provide eight steps to help you escape the narcissist in your life and find emotional freedom.

There is no substitute for finding a great, understanding, knowledgeable therapist to support you along the way. In fact, neither of us (your authors) could have survived without the support of insightful mental health professionals. But the eight steps described in the following chapters will help you begin the path to healing. It won't be easy. You'll need to see things for what they are, admit that you are traumatized and stuck, and be willing to cope with realizations that are tough to face. Even though the journey is not easy, you can be assured that you will have very few regrets after leaving a narcissist. Most people celebrate the day they "left their narcissist." Suffering with and then leaving a narcissist is a unique journey. Educating your-self about narcissism, recognizing the narcissistic abuse, and making the journey of self-discovery required to escape the narcissist's influ-ence is a powerful experience. As a result of the ordeal of being with a narcissist, you will be more insightful, more self-assured, and better equipped to surround yourself with positive, genuine people. There is definitely light at the end of the tunnel, and it is you who are shining!

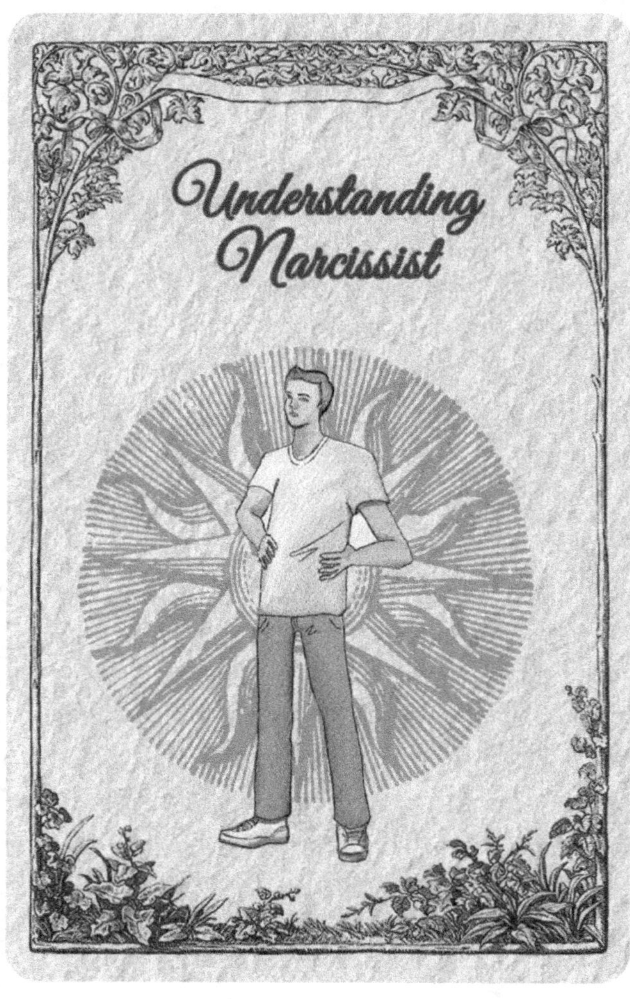

Understanding narcissism and its hold on your life is critical to eliminating it and distancing yourself from the narcissist. The good news is, if you've read this far, you probably have a pretty good understanding of narcissism and an awareness of the ways it has infected your life. At this point, you may feel that everyone is a narcissist (they're not.) But it is very important to know what you are up against.

NARCISSIST-PROOFING: IT BEGINS WITH BOUNDARIES

Narcissists blur and ignore boundaries. They will go anywhere, they will do anything that meets their emotional needs, and, frankly, they do not consider boundaries. They will embarrass you in public, and they enjoy doing so. They have no discretion, few limits to what they are willing to do or lines they are willing to cross. They are quite comfortable invading your personal space. They will seek out your emotional weaknesses and aim their attacks directly at those vulnerabilities. But first, they test and research and explore to find your limits, before they trample them. They start by trying to see what they can get away with, and then they will try a little more, and still more, and so on. And over time, sometimes a long period of time, you become aware that they're really in your personal space. They're talking to your friends and slandering you or working to affect the opinions others hold of you. They're on your Facebook page, they're calling your family or former lovers, they're invading your place of business. In effect, narcissists adhere only to the boundaries *they* set. They may very well have boundaries with others and may seem normal, acting as anything but a narcissist around them. That's why other people really like them. Their façade is very good. But with the object of their so-called affections, they have zero boundaries.

We can always establish boundaries for ourselves. Will the narcissist respect us after they're broken? Well, we already know that the narcissist won't respect anything, so forget about him or her. This is

about you. You have to set boundaries. Your narcissist claims he has PTSD because of you and is seeking therapy? Good for him. You almost have to laugh, yet it's anything but funny when you're in it.

So how do you set boundaries? You can start by not reacting or responding. Don't get excited or upset. That's what they want—to elicit responses. Don't give them the reactions they're looking for. Don't take the bait. Don't fight. You can't win. They're professionals at this.

You can say, "I don't think that's true," or acknowledge that the person spoke by saying, "I hear what you're saying," but don't get pulled down into the mud. Just say, "Got it," and that's it. That's responding without reacting. Don't engage. He can't fight if you aren't fighting. Don't acquiesce, and don't fight.

You can use the broken record technique, where you repeat yourself without getting drawn into the fight. "I heard you. I get it. I heard what you said. I'm listening." But don't agree to do anything.

Set rules for yourself—start with just three, and over time, the rules start becoming boundaries. For example, you can tell yourself, "I deserve not to be yelled at," "I deserve to be treated better," "I am entitled to express opinions and preferences without being criticized." Even if the narcissist is not treating you better right now, you are establishing rules. You may not yet be ready to walk out the door, but you do need to practice internal rules and boundaries: "I know I will not put up with being yelled at, even though I cannot do anything at this moment," or "I won't obey these abusive rules, but I need to be safe for just a bit more."

Also, of course, if the issue is physical safety, or if there is a chance of imminent harm, you may have to appease the narcissist. Safety is always first. In a threatening situation, inform family and friends, keep trusted people in the loop, keep a record of what's happening, and inform others of where you are at all times.

Setting a boundary for self-care is great. You have the right, even in a narcissistic relationship, to take care of yourself—to start some yoga, to improve your eating habits, to get some exercise—regardless of whether your little narcissist comes with you or not. Get a haircut, go to the dentist, go to the doctor's appointments you've been putting off. Read a book. Expand your horizons. Be good to yourself!

Taking care of yourself is a vital boundary to set because it leaves you better able to set additional boundaries. Another foundational boundary to set is the refusal to accept any kind of physical abuse or threat. You have the right to be safe. Don't hesitate to call the police, or whatever it takes, if you're under physical threat. Never do anything, even following the suggestions in this book, if you know it will lead to physical danger.

Never agree, internally, with the narcissist's ridiculous accusations and demands. Make sure there's a difference between what you're doing to placate or distance yourself from the narcissist and what you're doing in your own head. When caught in the cyclone of a narcissistic relationship, it is difficult to maintain all your boundaries. Maintain as many as possible.

Reaching out for assistance is also a form of boundary setting, even if it's only looking up information on the internet, joining a support group, or spending time with a trusted friend. You have the right to social and emotional support. Find a friend who understands, who has been there. Contact a friend who is not also a friend of the narcissist's. The narcissist may work to isolate you, may try to turn friends into flying monkeys.

The ultimate boundary is to leave, because the relationship costs you too much. We had someone in a group who said they would have been dead inside if they had waited any longer to leave. The death of the mind, soul, and spirit is not the only death. It can be a literal thing—we often see people trying to hurt themselves or getting physically sick from the relationship. That is never worth it.

Ultimately, we have the right to our own self-esteem, to feel good about ourselves. If we decide on the boundaries we want to set and then practice setting them and living by them, the boundaries become a reality, and the people in our lives will begin to respect them.

QUESTION: What's the most important thing to know about narcissists?

DR. FRED

That they are seriously dangerous. They are capable of tremendous, almost unbelievable damage to health, safety, relationships, and finances. The time spent with a narcissist will not end well. Leave as soon as you possibly can. If you can't, at least disengage to the best of your ability.

DR. ROBIN

They are very broken and damaged human beings. They will bring drama and heartache into your life. They cannot be trusted and will project their vileness onto close intimate partners that fall into their web of deceit and lies.

8

Hello, It's Me

Now it's time to turn your attention to yourself. Most individuals who feel stuck in a relationship with a narcissist find this step toward healing to be difficult. When immersed in a relationship with a narcissist, it feels as though your mind has been hijacked and all you can do is think about the narcissist. Why did they do this or that? Why are they treating me like this? And, of course, what did I do wrong?

Some individuals in relationships with narcissists have traits that feed the narcissist's pathological need for servile attention. One trait that feeds the narcissist's appetites is codependency. Note that the term *codependency* includes the word *dependency*. A person who has an unhealthy dependence on another for approval, guidance, and self-esteem may be said to be codependent. Codependency is a psychological condition in a relationship in which a person is controlled or manipulated by another who is affected by a pathology. Individuals who gain their sense of self by taking care of others, not upholding their boundaries, and people-pleasing become easy targets for narcissists.

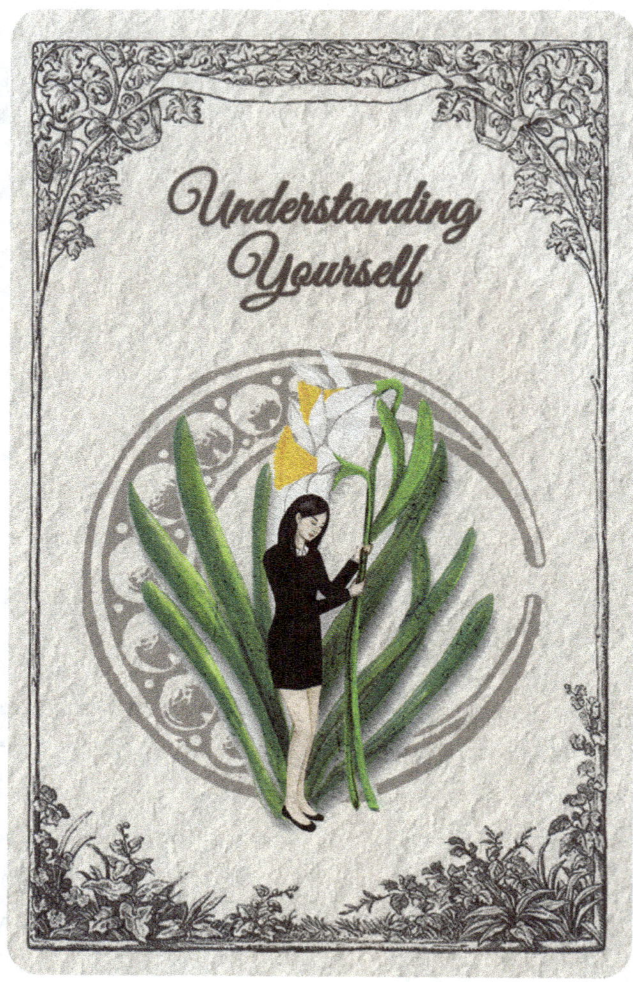

Narcissistic abuse, though, can occur with individuals who are not dependent on the narcissist to fulfill their sense of self. As revealed in the *2-Day Intensive Training on Narcissistic and Psychopathic Abuse* workbook by Sandra Brown, Claudia Paradise, and William Brennan, about 70 percent of all individuals who have been in a relationship with a narcissist are not considered to be emotionally codependent—but that leaves 30 percent who are.

The most important part of breaking free from the narcissist is understanding yourself: Why did you get involved and stay with the narcissist? What are the components of codependency? One important factor is individual susceptibility based on attachment style. Individuals in relationships with a narcissist, and the narcissists themselves, sometimes had early attachment difficulties with their primary caregivers—in other words, problems with forming healthy emotional bonds with caregivers and difficulties with trust and the acceptance of others as safe and available. When caregivers respond quickly and consistently, children learn that they can depend on the people who are responsible for them, which is the essential foundation for attachment. Experiencing inconsistent, addicted, emotionally absent, or downright abusive parenting leads to deficient attachment styles. Exploring the origin of unhealthy patterns of attachment is one reason that seeking therapy is vital for healing after a narcissist has thrown your world off-balance.

John Bowlby was a psychologist who conducted studies on attachment. According to Bowlby, attachment is an emotional bond with another person. An unhealthy attachment can be formed with a dysfunctional primary caregiver. A child may learn that crying, or any expression of strong emotion, will lead to rejection, and so will grow up to have difficulty expressing feelings openly because of a fear of retribution. Bowlby believed that dysfunctional parents can "mystify" a child's legitimate concerns. For example, if a child approaches a parent with "I am sad," it would be a negation of the child's true feelings to respond with "No, you're not. You're just selfish!"

There are several dysfunctional attachment styles. Children with *ambivalent* attachment become very distressed when, for example, a parent leaves the room. As a result of poor parental availability, these children cannot depend on their primary caregivers to be there when they need them. Children with an *avoidant* attachment tend to avoid parents or caregivers, showing no difference in preference between a caregiver and a complete stranger. They have been punished for relying on a caregiver and will learn to avoid seeking help in the future. Children with *disorganized* attachment have no idea what to do to please their parents and so display a wide variety of disorganized behaviors.

Anxious attachment is probably the best explanation for why people stay with abusive partners. A child will often cling to an emotionally unavailable or destructive parent in a sad attempt to obtain the nurturing they require. Although attachment styles displayed in adulthood are not necessarily the same as those seen in infancy, early attachments can have a serious impact on later relationships. Adults who were securely attached in childhood tend to have good self-esteem, strong romantic relationships, and the ability to self-disclose to others. Anxious attachment leads to adult dependency issues, poor self-esteem, expectations of low standards of treatment in relationships, people-pleasing, and difficulty setting and keeping boundaries. These are the same traits that can make someone feel vulnerable, stuck, and lost when dealing with a narcissist.

According to Ross Rosenberg, a psychotherapist and founder of the Self-Love Recovery Institute, all relationships have a certain level of codependency. The problem is when it's the main feature of a relationship and leads to high levels of drama. Codependency means that one partner will give himself or herself to the other without any boundaries, without any filters or limitations. Narcissists thrive on having this kind of unconditional partner. They initially respond with signs of affection, attention, and care. At this point, the relationship feels perfectly balanced and harmonious. But the narcissist will start to want more. Even if the other person gives them every part of themselves, the narcissist will feel like something is missing. Over time, what they receive won't satisfy them anymore. They'll start to ask, or demand, more and more.

The codependent will end up feeling as if they're not good enough. They'll feel that maybe the other person doesn't really need them.

That will fill them up with insecurity and they'll try to give more and more, but eventually they'll start to complain about their partner's indifference. The codependent may want to keep being controlled because it remains a form of attention and, in a distorted way, may be experienced as "caring." The narcissistic person will have a desperate need for their adoring follower.

We can become addicted to our narcissistic partner, with devastating results. In the beginning, love bombing and all, the interplay gives a wonderfully pleasant, euphoric feeling. Even though the pleasant feeling starts to go away as time goes by, and suffering takes its place, we neither accept that the pleasure from the beginning is gone nor that it wasn't genuine in the first place. We compulsively seek that initial, amazing sensation. The intense conflict, the roller-coaster ride of emotional highs and lows, the bucket-list level of excitement, are always present with a narcissist and lead to a cycle of addiction. The drama and the cycle of conflict, whether positive or negative, create adrenaline and brain stimulation whose absence mimics withdrawal from drugs or alcohol.

The hallmark of a narcissist is the "cycle of abuse." The first few phases of the cycle consist of the love bombing phase, then the narcissist becoming emotionally distant, controlling, demeaning, devaluing, and ultimately rejecting. The cycle returns to the love bombing, grandiose promises, and future faking all over again. The cycle of abuse is the perfect mechanism for addiction. The abused partner knows that the narcissist is capable of affection and attention, "if only I learn to do the right thing." The cycle of abuse is emotionally damaging and can even be deadly.

The unusually deep bond we feel with the narcissist is referred to as a "trauma bond." It's a connection with another person based not on mutual respect, love, true affection, or a deep sense of togetherness but rather on an underlying addiction to a narcissistic partner. We are constantly hoping to regain the feelings associated with the love bombing phase. The desire to feel the affection associated with the love bombing phase is intense, but it is more accurately a pathological need. We find ourselves losing our identity in the process of trying to make the relationship work.

Dopamine and oxytocin are the two neurotransmitters that play a large role in trauma bonding. Dopamine is a neurotransmitter in the brain that creates feelings of pleasure. Individuals in emotionally abusive relationships experience moments of calm, with love bombing and future faking from their abuser. Oxytocin is a neuropeptide and hormone that has been termed the "love and cuddle" hormone because it's released during physical intimacy. When both hormones are released over and over and are cycled with intermittent abuse, a bond with the abuser will be strengthened.

When the relationship with a narcissist ends and there is a withdrawal of dopamine and oxytocin, the individual is left with the same neurocircuitry that is associated with drug dependency. There is similar chemistry in healthy relationships as well; however, the intensity of emotions and the inconsistency and cyclic nature of narcissistic abuse creates stronger chemical bonds. In many cases, narcissists are exciting figures. They can be very compelling, dynamic, "living on the edge" characters. Our brains miss the pageantry and grandiosity of the narcissist. This loss is often what is responsible for the individual repeatedly going back to the abuser; they need to get a surge of oxytocin and dopamine to feel more in balance and regain homeostasis.

In addition to this neurochemical withdrawal we feel, we also succumb to the power of intermittent reinforcement. The narcissist sometimes shows love and affection. Once in a great while, seemingly without pattern, the narcissist will be sweet, compelling, sensual, and generous. Behavioral psychologists have known for a century that if you randomly and intermittently reinforce (reward) an individual, the person will engage in the strongest of behaviors to get that reward again. Even a rat in a cage will incessantly press a bar that releases a food pellet if you only occasionally, and randomly, distribute the actual food. The narcissist uses these patterns of intermittent reinforcement. Most of the time they are cruel and mean, but now and then they will "breadcrumb" their target with kind behavior, usually in the form of attention or gifts or compliments, and possibly a dose of future faking. So there is continuous anticipation of reward and hope for good things to happen. Research psychologists have demonstrated that intermittent reinforcement results in intense behavioral responses, and the narcissist is instinctually aware of this.

All these addictive qualities of the relationship with a narcissist contribute to the extreme difficulties involved with leaving and staying away from them. This is why the best policy to use in leaving the narcissist, as in quitting a drug, is often "cold turkey" or "no contact." It's extremely difficult to leave an abusive relationship without the help of a professional therapist who understands this behavioral dynamic.

Even after you have left the narcissist, you are likely to be haunted by flashbacks. Flashbacks of the abuse and horrible manipulation can be unbearable, but pleasant flashbacks of incredibly good times can be even worse. You are desperately trying to forget about the relationship, and you find yourself smiling and feeling that thrill of adrenaline again when you remember a great experience. You may feel guilty after a flashback of a pleasurable encounter with the narcissist. The "addiction" may be reactivated involuntarily, and it's infuriating.

Peter Walker, a marriage and family therapist specializing in conflict resolution in relationships, suggests that effective recovery from an abusive narcissist requires the gradual reduction of emotional flashbacks. Over time we become more and more proficient at managing them and alleviating unnecessary states of activation; this in turn results in flashbacks occurring less frequently and being diminished in duration and intensity. Flashbacks can also trigger several kinds of instant trauma responses, the same responses encountered during the actual abuse: fight (the impulse to attack, defeat, and overcome the threat), flight (the desire to run away, escape, or hide from the danger), freeze (the feeling of being immobilized, helpless, trapped, or stuck) or fawn (the desire to placate, please, and accommodate to make the danger stop). The freeze and fawn responses may be responsible for Stockholm syndrome, a tendency to identify with the aggressor. Any of these trauma responses to flashbacks can be debilitating. The reactions occur even when there is no tangible threat, and they increase anxiety, stress levels, and depression.

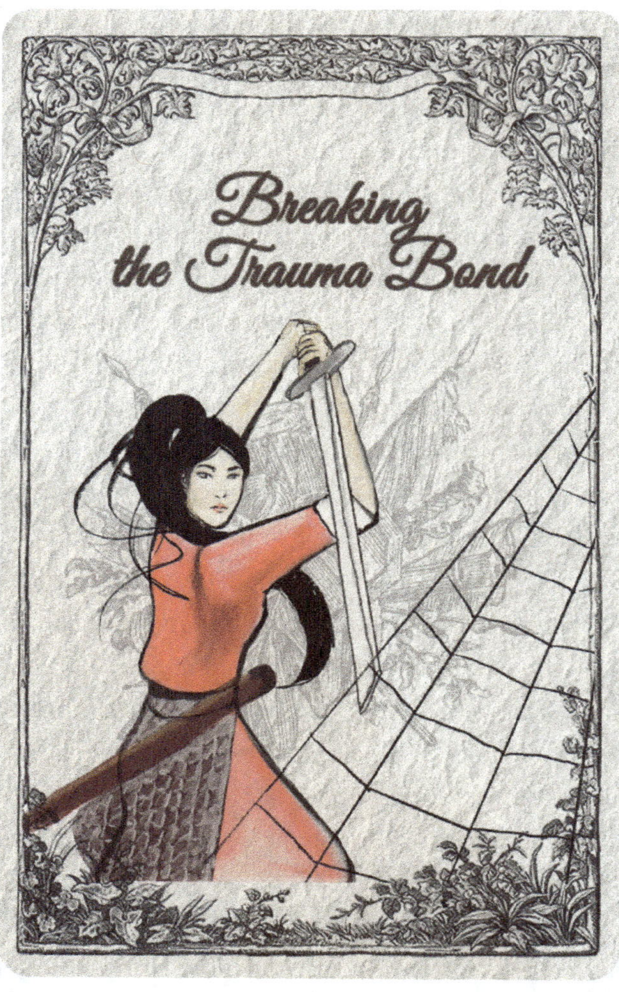

One sign that we are recovering from narcissistic abuse, according to Walker, is a gradual increase in our ability to relax after an inappropriate fight, flight, freeze, or fawn response. There is also an increase in our ability to use our fight, flight, freeze, and fawn instincts in healthy non-self-destructive ways, so that we only fight back when under real attack, only flee when odds are insurmountable, only freeze when we need to go into acute observer mode, and only fawn when it is appropriate to be self-sacrificing. Other important methods for counteracting the traumatic effects of the narcissist are learning relaxation techniques to lessen the anxiety, engaging in physical exercise to stay generally healthy and generate natural adrenaline, seeking social support, gaining awareness of triggers, and practicing self-compassion. It is also important not to judge your trauma responses or feel ashamed of them.

Walker advises, "Recognize that these responses, at one point, served as your understanding of the best way to cope with a threat. With an open mind, gain an understanding that our trauma responses may not seem to always be useful in protecting us, the way they did in the past, in current nonthreatening situations."

The pathway to recovering from narcissistic abuse is difficult. You were certainly abused, taken advantage of, duped, manipulated, lied to . . . you were victimized. But you are not a victim.

Understanding the narcissist is step one. Understanding yourself and your role in this relationship and what makes you vulnerable to the narcissist is step two, and a great step toward freedom from your narcissist.

While none of us wants to dwell on our more challenging personality traits, being able to be honest with ourselves about our traits is a big step toward being free of the narcissist in our lives. Ask yourself whether you feel responsible for the happiness of the narcissist. Do you suffer from low self-esteem, anxiety, and/or stress? Do you have difficulty setting boundaries? Do you fixate on your mistakes? Do you feel the need to be a caretaker of others? If you answered yes to some of these questions, consider seeking help from a qualified professional with experience in treating people who have been the targets of narcissists.

DR. FRED

That I could do it. I was not alone. Other people had done this before me, and in much more dire circumstances than mine. I had the resources, I learned what I was up against, and I took action. Thank God.

DR. ROBIN

That I could do anything I put my mind to. I was strong, and even when I had bad days and awful feelings, I didn't let that stop me from moving forward. My strengths are my problem-solving and my intuition. This combination of personality traits and drive helped me immensely when I decided to leave.

9

Victimized, Not Victim

STEP 3. DON'T BE A VICTIM!

Targets of narcissists who have been emotionally battered and beaten down may tend to view themselves as victims. This is not easy to overcome, because it challenges their core value system. In order to heal, they need to take into account their role in the relationship and take responsibility for their own actions.

We cannot change the narcissist's needs, behavior, speech, or actions. We can only control our own, and some of what is suggested here will be difficult and uncomfortable. Rather than trying to convince a narcissist to feel or act differently, we can respond in ways that move us from a victim mentality to one of radical acceptance. Rather than trying to reason with the narcissist, we can say, "I'm sorry you feel that way" or "I hear what you're saying." How about this: "Your anger is not my responsibility." This throws the ball back into the narcissist's court. Much of what narcissists say is bait, some version of carrot-and-stick, good cop bad cop, Jekyll-Hyde tactics designed to sap your ability to resist and herd you into his or her sick, pathological universe of compliance.

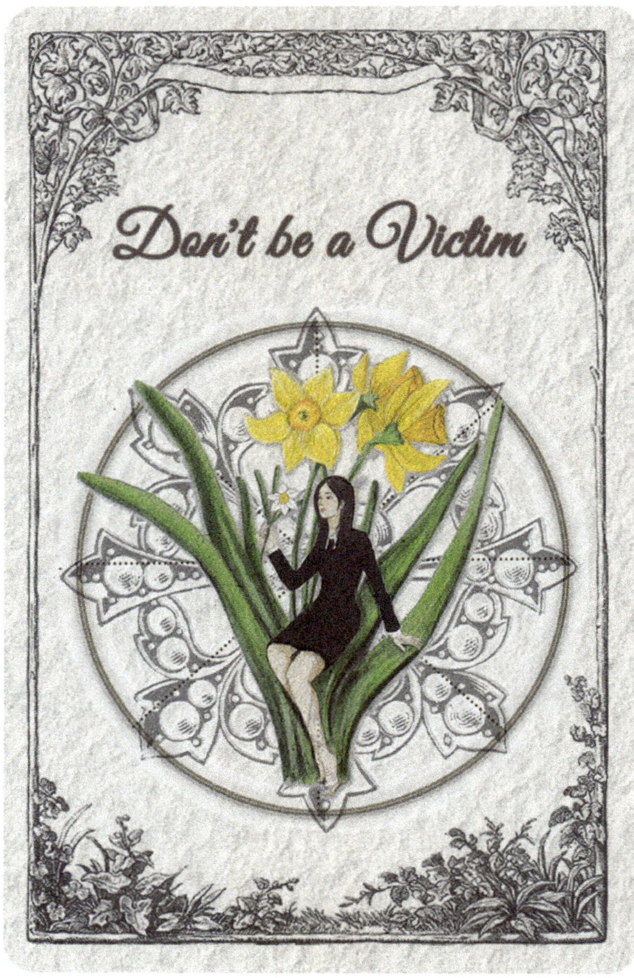

Accepting your current situation does not mean that you will stop planning to leave. Acceptance is just a recognition of the reality of the circumstances: the narcissist will not change, things will not get better, and it's time to move forward. Realizing that you are not a victim but that you were *victimized* will help you develop emotional maturity and put the best version of yourself out into the world. You get to decide what is important to you and aim your energy at that. You get to decide what and whom you want in your world! These kinds of empowering responses will get you there. You have the power to be the arbiter of your own life and happiness. You are good enough, smart enough, capable enough. And with the right tools, you can and will do this.

What we are talking about here is emerging from the darkness of the narcissist's shadow, learning emotional maturity and self-love, and becoming the high-functioning adult you were meant to be.

During this period of healing and recovery, dating is not usually recommended. You will need to date yourself, love yourself, heal your inner child, be your own partner and your own loving parent. If the opportunity to enter an emotionally healthy and genuinely loving relationship should arise, and you personally feel you are healed enough to handle it, it's hard to argue against seizing the opportunity.

Finding your "self" is always central to the recovery process. You will become aware of what self-care is to you and will habituate that care. What do you love to do? Self-care might be taking walks on the beach and learning to say no to people who devalue you and drain your energy.

You will know that you are not the victim when you feel grounded and self-assured, and you feel as if you can walk into a room and have a presence. That presence is the real you. Energy is everything here. At this step in the healing process, you will have gotten rid of, or are able to manage, toxic people in your life. There will also be none or very little of the narcissist left in your life and few physical manifestations or mental ruminations about your (former) narcissist. When you get a hoover (a narcissist who attempts to suck you back into the maelstrom of drama), you are able to ignore the narcissist's goal and throw that negative energy back out into the universe.

The idea that the narcissistic abuse you have suffered is in any way your fault is ridiculous. Although possible, it is not necessarily true that you are codependent or an "empath" or have unresolved abandonment or attachment issues, or that you had narcissistic parents or a bad childhood. It's very probable that you are completely normal and got suckered by a professional, pathological manipulator. The narcissist may have zeroed in on certain personality traits, but often those focused on are actually positive and healthy. Don't lose them in your struggle to escape the narcissist!

Recent research suggests that you are likely to be agreeable, trusting, warm and approachable, good at finding solutions, kind, forgiving, compassionate, generous, optimistic, tolerant of differing opinions, willing to compromise, and loyal. These are very positive, healthy, and psychologically normal personality traits. You should be proud of yourself. Treasure those traits, protect them, and never for a minute believe that anything was your fault. Don't allow the narcissist to change your wonderful personality. Learn from the experience and don't "cast your pearls before swine." In other words, don't give your best to people who do not appreciate or deserve it.

BOUNDARIES, RULES, AND STANDARDS

Narcissists will do almost anything to push your boundaries: invade your space, contact your friends without consent, dig up your past unexpectedly, and so forth. Maintaining a consistent set of boundaries, things you simply will not put up with or things you just refuse to do (like apologize when you know you did nothing wrong) is essential. But what happens when you have no choice or when you are forced by the narcissist to say or do things that are not in your comfort zone? Sometimes the best we can do is maintain a strong set of internal rules. Even while complying with the narcissist's demands, we can think to ourselves, "I'm doing this to keep the peace. When I get out of this situation, I will never be like this again." We can internally repeat strongly held beliefs and standards, like "I would never apologize for something that is not my responsibility."

QUESTION: What helped you transform from being a victim to being someone who was victimized?

DR. FRED

Learning the vocabulary surrounding narcissistic abuse, knowing I was not alone, and admitting that I was in an abusive relationship. These things gave me a lot of strength. Personally, I did not want to allow the narcissist to prevent me from moving forward with my life.

DR. ROBIN

When you finally realize that you've been with a narcissist and the pieces of the puzzle in your life come together and make sense (e.g., "Aah, that's why I felt confused for so long"), you begin to imagine your life without the drama, cognitive dissonance, and feelings of shame. I made a deal with myself to always be my best self, be positive, be mindful of living in the present and cognizant of planning my future. This is quite the opposite of the victim mentality. I knew I had to take responsibility for my life in order to move forward.

10

All You Need Is Self-Love

STEP 4. SELF-LOVE IS SELF-CARE

Self-love means prioritizing our own hopes, needs, and desires. Sounds simple, right? But we who have been in relationships with narcissists have been taught to prioritize the narcissist at the expense of ourselves, and often we have been taught to do so by professionals. The PsychCentral blog post "33 Ways to Love Yourself More" tells us that self-love can be as simple as allowing ourselves to make mistakes. It starts with awareness. If we are burned out, we need to rest; if we are hurt, we need to nurture ourselves; if we are afraid, we need to ensure our safety. We should love ourselves at least as much as and maybe a little more than we love others. Is this selfish? No! To tend to a child on an airplane in which the pressure has dropped, we need to first put the oxygen mask on ourselves. Only then, only when we are safe, are we fit to care for the child. Caring for ourselves allows us to care for others.

Self-love can include eating nutritious meals, getting enough sleep, exercising, and managing our stress levels. Self-love is a self-fulfilling exercise—the more we eat nutritiously, get enough sleep, exercise, and manage stress, the better able we are to do these very things, in an upward-spiraling cycle. Self-love also creates resiliency. We will better cope with challenging circumstances when we care for ourselves.

Having an awareness that we cannot always fix ourselves might mean booking time with a therapist. Self-care might mean bringing in a specialist of sorts. Therapy may be the ultimate expression of self-care.

We can be our own champions. Now that we have learned how to identify narcissistic behaviors, we can maintain awareness and vigilance. Many of us grew up with or have had experiences in which we learned that we were not safe. Either we were never taught to feel safe or we were in unsafe relationships. Now, armed with knowledge, awareness, and tools, we can keep ourselves safe, and once we know we are safe, we can trust our feelings. We deserve to feel fulfilled. We deserve to feel loved. We deserve to love ourselves. We deserve to treasure ourselves.

If we feel as though there is something missing, something *is* missing, and that is not our fault. If we feel disconnected, that is not our fault. Narcissistic relationships may have left us feeling shamed and afraid of abandonment. That is not our fault.

Lisa Romano, author and social media expert on narcissistic relationships, suggests that our reactions to our traumas are natural and that we can consciously choose to focus on the light of our true selves and to affirm ourselves. We can practice seeing ourselves as part of a great reality, of all that is, as valid, as enough—as divine. Whatever our spiritual or religious point of view, she is showing us that our minds and bodies are absolutely there for us, have been with us since before we were born, and we can do the same; we can be there for ourselves by validating ourselves with intention. Caring for ourselves will nurture a natural healing process.

Examples of self-care can be found almost anywhere. Janice, a woman who was raised by a highly narcissistic mother, was convinced that she herself was exhibiting many narcissistic tendencies. She found great comfort and inspiration in a book that is nearly one hundred years old: *How to Win Friends and Influence People* by Dale Carnegie. Janice explained that simply following the clear, systematic steps and relatable examples suggested in the book made her a better person.

Talk with a qualified therapist about various modalities and, if you feel they are for you, read, explore, and learn. You get to decide what is right for your healing journey and your healed future.

The relationships that should have filled us up—our families of origin, our significant others—may not have done so. We may grow up parented by narcissists and lack the elemental tools for feeling safe, for validation. Or we may be targeted and preyed upon by a narcissist and lose our sense of self-fulfillment.

We have learned here how to find our way out of narcissistic relationships, what to do and not do with narcissists, and how to recognize them before we become enmeshed with these dangerous, damaged, pathological people. We have free will. We have the power to choose love. We have the power to heal ourselves, which may include using affirmations, reading, meditating, and, if necessary, finding and vetting clinical help.

So how do we guarantee ourselves a fulfilled, happy, joyous life experience? By investing time, understanding, love, respect, gratitude, appreciation, forgiveness, and abundant energy in ourselves. The more we do this, the happier and more fulfilling our experiences will be.

After you leave the primary narcissist in your life, you will probably become more aware of other manipulative, controlling, and abusive individuals. You can apply all you have learned to cope with (or just avoid) these people. Self-care is your best defense. Self-care is a skill, and success will require practice and a little bit of trial and error regarding which methods work best for you and your specific situation. The following are techniques to protect yourself against narcissists and reach a state of confidence and peace.

ASSERTIVENESS

The development of assertiveness is closely related to the ability to set boundaries. Assertiveness is not "getting what you want," but rather expressing your feelings and thoughts accurately to others. Becoming more assertive may confuse or anger the narcissist you are dealing with. He or she may react negatively to the change in your attitude or perceive the "new you" as a challenge. Be aware of techniques the narcissist may use to disregard or avoid your concerns. The narcissist will deny your rights by doing any of the following:

1. Changing the subject
2. Responding with a strong display of emotion (including anger)
3. Joking or making fun of your requests or expressions of opinion
4. Trying to make you feel guilty about requests or thoughts
5. Criticizing or questioning the legitimacy of your requests or ideas
6. Asking why you want what you asked for
7. Gaslighting, denying previous actions, blaming you

It may take some practice and experimentation to see which of the techniques discussed below will work best in your situation.

Regardless of what assertiveness techniques you use, you will want to identify your personal rights. Practice the elements of this personal "Bill of Rights" first, every day, until the time arrives when you are completely free of the narcissist. Post this list on your refrigerator, or in a safe place, and read the items every day. Consider adding a few more to customize the list.

Personal Bill of Rights

1. I have the right to personal space and privacy in my home.
2. I have the right to take my own time and use it however I want to.
3. I have the right to believe, think, and feel whatever I want.
4. I have the right to get as much rest and sleep as I need.
5. I have the right to live in a calm environment.
6. I have the right to ask what you want.
7. I have the right to say no to requests or demands I can't meet.
8. I have the right to express my feelings, positive or negative.
9. I have the right to change my mind.
10. I have the right to make mistakes and not to have to be perfect.
11. I have the right to determine my priorities.
12. I have the right not to be responsible for others' behavior, actions, feelings, or problems.
13. I have the right to expect honesty from others.
14. I have the right to be angry at someone I love.
15. I have the right to feel scared and to say I'm afraid.
16. I have the right not to give reasons for my decisions or my behavior.
17. I have the right to make decisions based on my feelings and intuitions.
18. I have the right to be playful and frivolous and not take what others say so seriously.
19. I have the right to be healthier than those around me.

20. I have the right to be in a nonabusive environment.
21. I have the right to be in a healthy, loving, and nurturing relationship.
22. I have the right to be loved, respected, and appreciated.
23. I have the right to make friends and be comfortable around people.

Broken Record Technique

Practice using this technique when meeting with resistance or indifference. The broken record technique consists of stating repeatedly what you want in a calm, direct manner with the persistence of a broken record. You can use this technique in situations where you're unwilling to do what the other person suggests or when you want to do something that the other person disagrees with. Using this technique, you stay focused on what you want and don't give in to the other person's will. You simply state what you want as many times as you need to, without change or embellishment. Do *not* back down or give reasons justifying your opinion. Start with "I want . . ." or "I would like . . ." This technique is used to get your request across even in the face of resistance or evasiveness. It is not intended to foster intimate, long-term communication, but rather to make sure your requests receive clear responses. Start small, with less crucial issues, and work your way up. In the following example, you wish to go to the mall by yourself just to have some private time.

Narcissist: "I'm going to come with you."

You: "I'm going to the mall by myself this time."

Narcissist: "We always go together. What's going on?"

You: "I would like to go to the mall alone."

Narcissist: "Didn't I help you last time we went? We had fun!"

You: "I would like to spend some time at the mall by myself."

Narcissist: "Well, I can just drive you and hang out at the Apple store."

You: "I don't want company this time, thank you. I want to go to the mall alone."

Narcissist: "Maybe you and I can go to dinner after? Let me find a great restaurant."

You: "No, thank you. I am going to the mall myself."

Narcissist: "You've never done that before."

You: "I understand this is different. But I would like to go myself."

Narcissist: "I'll have to get dinner or cook myself tonight if you go."

You: "Okay."

Narcissist: "Is there something wrong?"

You: "No. Nothing is wrong. I would just like to go to the mall by myself."

Narcissist: "Fine!"

Of course, when dealing with narcissists it doesn't always go as well or as smoothly as in this example. And it's hard not to feel silly repeating the same sentence over and over. With practice, however, the technique can be very effective.

The Very Popular Gray Rock Approach

The gray rock method is a strategy to use when interacting with manipulative or abusive individuals of all kinds. It involves becoming as unresponsive as possible to the abusive person's behavior, similar to acting like a neutral gray rock—solid, strong, but emotionally uninvolved and nonreactive. The gray rock method involves communicating with the narcissist in an uninteresting way and may include the following:

Avoiding interactions with the abusive person

Keeping unavoidable interactions very brief

Giving short or one-word answers to questions

Communicating in a factual, unemotional way

The aim is to cause the narcissist to lose interest and stop the antagonistic behavior, so as to protect your own emotional well-being. You can use this tactic if interactions with the abusive person are unavoidable. It is helpful, but it is not a viable long-term strategy. It may be enough to deter some narcissists, but it also carries the risk of escalating aggressive behavior. When communicating with the narcissist, try to do the following:

Be very brief: Give short answers to questions, such as "yes," "no," or "I don't know."

Be factual: Use simple, true statements during conversations and avoid disclosing personal opinions or information unnecessarily. This keeps the conversation impersonal.

Avoid emotional engagement: This can be difficult, particularly if a person is acting in a threatening or antagonistic way. To remain detached from the conversation, try focusing on breathing, and avoid making eye contact.

Maintain privacy: Avoid sharing personal information with them, including on social media.

Fogging

Fogging is another technique to use with someone who is being critical of you. It involves agreeing in part with the criticism. You outwardly agree with some part of the criticism in a noncommittal way even though you don't believe all of it. You need to do this in a calm, quiet tone of voice without being defensive or sarcastic. If you don't agree with the specific criticism, you can agree with the general principle behind it and simply say, "You may be right." When you agree with people, they have little tendency to come back and criticize or argue with you further. Fogging effectively stops communication before the other person can escalate a disagreement. The narcissist is hearing what they want to hear. In the following example, the narcissist is criticizing the way you look, and you are going to agree with the other person just enough to let them think you will follow their advice. This time, let's assume the narcissist is a parent:

Narcissist: "Your skirt is kind of short. Don't you think you should wear it longer? The style is longer skirts now."

You: "You're probably right. The style is longer skirts now."

Narcissist: "I think that if your hair was shorter, it might be easier to take care of."

You: "You could be right. Good idea. Short hair is easier."

Narcissist: "You'd look much more feminine if you used lip liner."

You: "You're right. I hadn't thought about it. I might look more feminine with lip liner."

Narcissist: "You really should set a good example for your daughter. She copies you."

You: "Yes, she does copy me."

Narcissist: "Let's go out to lunch."

You: "I'm ready, let's go."

Like the broken record, fogging is useful in situations where you want to minimize communication. You don't want to listen to advice and you don't want to argue. Fogging is not always good for situations with partners or friends where you wish to keep communication open and give the other an opportunity to get his or her feelings out.

Defusing

Defusing is a good technique to use when the other person becomes angry or hostile. It's a bit like defusing a bomb. It's a delaying tactic that is best used when someone responds to your assertive request with intense anger or any other extreme display of emotion. In close, healthy relationships, it's important to allow other people to express their strong feelings. When dealing with a narcissist, however, it's often unlikely that he or she will be open to hearing your assertive request. In these cases, it's better to say, "I can see that you're very upset—let's discuss this later." This communication technique is used when emotions begin to get extreme. When you sense that anger or hostility from the other person is getting out of hand, try this:

You: "I'd like to have my sister visit for the holidays."

Your spouse: "What!? Not again! You're going to do this to me again? I absolutely won't have it! No way!"

You: "I can see that you're upset, and I can even understand. Let's talk about it another time."

Simplification

When asking for something or making any kind of request of a narcissist, keep it simple. Use one or two easy-to-understand sentences. Avoid asking for more than one thing at a time. This will have the effect of getting the other person to focus on what you are saying, so they won't perceive your important request as just another "list of complaints."

Reflection

An important aspect of being assertive is your ability to say no to requests that you don't want to meet without feeling guilty. There are some situations when you may want to give the other person some explanation for turning down a request:

Acknowledge the other person's request by repeating it (rephrasing).

Explain your reason for declining the request.

Say no without apologizing.

Suggest an alternative proposal.

The "I" Statement

In a healthy, functioning relationship, the "I" statement method is a way of deepening understanding and communication. In a pathological relationship, this traditional advice may work, but do not expect the narcissist to understand or feel what you are going through. It's just a distraction technique with a narcissist. These types of statements are used only to avoid putting your partner on the defensive or blaming the other person for the problem (even when it is their fault). Practice beginning sentences with the following:

"I would like . . ."

"I want to . . ."

"I would appreciate it if . . ."

"It would make me feel great if . . ."

"I need more . . ."

"It would mean a lot to me if . . ."

Nonverbal Assertiveness

Practice nonverbal assertiveness when asking for something or turning down an unreasonable request:

Maintain eye contact. Face the person you are speaking with.

Be aware of good posture.

Adapt an "open" posture.

Speak slowly, calmly, and deliberately.

Take your time in formulating a response.

Make a list of what needs to be communicated before discussions.

Self-Reinforcement

Give yourself reinforcement after you have successfully acted assertively, even if the outcome was not exactly what you wanted. It is very important to be "self-rewarding." It encourages you to try again and protects you from being overly affected by situations out of your control. Rewards do not have to be monetary. Try listening to a favorite song, playing a game, or calling a long-distance friend.

MORE IDEAS

Take your time responding to the narcissist. Think and clarify what you want to say before responding to a request (for example, "I'll let you know by the end of the week," or "I'll think about it and tell you tomorrow morning"). Don't apologize. When you apologize for saying no, you give the narcissist the message that you're not sure your own needs are just as important as theirs. Be specific. It's important to be very specific in stating what you will and won't do, even when you do agree to do something. Face the person and maintain good eye contact. Speak in a calm but firm tone of voice. Avoid becoming emotional. You may feel the impulse to offer something else after turning down a specific request. Make sure that your offer comes out of genuine desire rather than guilt. Ask specifically for exactly what you want, or the person you're addressing may misunderstand. Instead of saying, "I would like you to come home by a reasonable hour," specify, for example, "I would like you to come home by midnight." Avoid using "you" statements. Statements that are threatening ("You'll do this or else") or coercive ("You *have* to . . .") will put a narcissist on the defensive and decrease the likelihood of your getting what you need.

ASSERTIVENESS BEYOND THE NARCISSIST

Moving beyond the abusive relationship, it is important to realize that assertiveness is on a continuum ranging from passivity to aggressiveness. Passivity involves letting things go, or "not sweating the small stuff." Of course, being too passive will lead to others taking advantage of you. Being assertive is usually a satisfying and ego-boosting approach, but there are times when more active responses are in order: insisting on speaking with the manager when dissatisfied, refusing to comply with unreasonable demands, or calling authorities when threatened. Assertiveness training can assist you in recognizing your capabilities in moving up or down the spectrum of possible reactions.

An interesting twist on assertiveness is to say "thank you" instead of "I'm sorry." Instead of apologizing for being late, thank people for their patience. Instead of lamenting a mistake, thank a colleague for helping you fix it. Instead of apologizing for speaking, voice appreciation for the people listening. It can shift your mindset from one of timidity and submission to one of confidence and empowerment. Research shows that by saying "thank you" instead of "sorry," your conversations become more about appreciation, which helps boost the self-esteem and satisfaction of the people on the receiving end of your words as well. This makes "thank you" better not only for you but for those around you.

PRO ASSERTIVENESS TIP

Learn to accept compliments. We often deny or negate compliments. If someone says, "That's a nice shirt," we may be inclined to respond, "This old thing? It's nothing special." That ends the conversation and diminishes the compliment-giver's opinion too. It would be better to say, "Oh, thank you!" That's acknowledging the compliment. But *accepting* the compliment is even better and promotes further communication: "Oh, thank you for noticing. I like it too. I got it at J.Crew." Accepting, or at least acknowledging, compliments is an act of assertiveness and will lead to improved self-esteem over time.

Identifying and internalizing your personal rights is also a necessary first step in regaining your sense of self. Effective assertiveness techniques enhance communication in healthy relationships. They are used to avoid conflict and can backfire when dealing with narcissists. You will need to use a little trial and error.

Being in a narcissistic relationship, especially a long-term one, will inevitably lead to experiencing psychological symptoms very similar to PTSD (post-traumatic stress disorder) or complex PTSD. These emotional consequences may persist long after you leave the narcissist.

You are very likely to experience several symptoms of anxiety and depression:

1. Numbness or tingling
2. Increased forgetfulness or lower concentration
3. Inability to relax
4. Fear of the worst happening
5. Dizziness, faintness, or light-headedness
6. Heart pounding, racing
7. Difficulty falling asleep or remaining asleep
8. Nervousness
9. Feelings of choking
10. Hands trembling or generally shaky
11. Terror, fear of harm or death
12. Fear of losing control
13. Difficulty breathing
14. Increased irritability
15. Indigestion or abdominal discomfort
16. Double-checking things more than necessary
17. Significant changes in appetite or weight
18. Sweating (not because of heat)
19. Distraction, inability to concentrate

The only way to start eliminating the stress for good is to leave the narcissist. Fortunately, there are several effective techniques for addressing the anxiety symptoms themselves.

AWARENESS OF STRESSFUL THOUGHTS

Reduce "stress-think." Although dealing with a narcissist is definitely one of the most stressful experiences imaginable, we still may have a habit of making the little molehills of life into mountains. Very often it is the things we say to ourselves that make a situation unnecessarily stressful. These "self-statements" or irrational beliefs can be instrumental in increasing stress and anxiety, lowering our attention span, and distracting us from achieving our goals. You may find some of the beliefs presented here to be very difficult to let go of, but holding on to them is self-defeating and may place unnecessarily stressful demands on an already crazy situation. It is a good idea to have high standards, ethical concerns about the world, and lofty goals. However, you may need to focus most of your energy on personal recovery at this time. Be particularly aware of extreme internal expressions such as "must," "always," "have to," and "terrible," "awful," or "disastrous."

Being with a narcissist is a hellish nightmare of irrationality. There is no way to sugarcoat it. But we can apply more rational thinking as much as we are able. Here are some common stress-thinks, along with alternative ways of viewing events:

My current situation is permanent and is not likely to change. (As bad or unfortunate as things may be right now, it is more productive to focus on activities that may make the situation better. Situations do change, and there is a great deal of truth to the saying, "Negative events are often opportunities in disguise.")

I must be loved and approved by every significant person in my life, and if I'm not, it's terrible. (It would be more productive to concentrate on self-respect, on winning approval for practical purposes, and on loving instead of being loved.)

I should be very anxious about events that are uncertain or potentially dangerous. (It would be better to face the danger or fear and render it harmless, and when that is impossible, accept the inevitable. Worrying will usually not help; action will. Most things that we worry about never actually happen!)

I am not worthwhile unless I am thoroughly competent, adequate, and achieving at all times. (It is more advisable to accept oneself as an imperfect creature with human limitations and faults. Retire from being manager of the universe!)

I should be comfortable and without pain at all times. (There's seldom gain without pain, and nothing of value is accomplished without risk. Replacement thought: I can tolerate this discomfort, although I may never like it.)

Stress comes from external pressure, and I can't control or change my feelings. Other people and events can ruin my day. (Distress is largely caused by the view one takes of conditions. You have enormous control over destructive emotions if you choose to believe that feelings are not "caused" by others but are a reaction from you. You control how your day turns out.)

My past is the cause of my present problems; because these events were strong influences on me, they will continue to be so. (One can learn from past experiences while not being overly attached to or prejudiced by them. The past has an influence, but it does not control you.)

Stress-think puts pressure on us to perform, gives us unrealistic expectations, and distorts our view of the events and interpersonal relationships around us. We already had the narcissist do that for us! Take some time to examine the thoughts, beliefs, and things you say to yourself that increase anxiety. Try to practice alternatives to your stressful thoughts. It may be a good idea to have someone who knows you well assist you in this exercise. They may be more objective and less caught up in the emotions of the situation.

POSITIVE AND NEGATIVE AFFIRMATIONS

Learn to use affirmations, or "coping statements." Coping statements are things we say to ourselves when we are in difficult situations. They are designed to replace irrational or stress-producing notions that we sometimes automatically call to mind. If you find yourself becoming stressful over something, refer to this list and read the statements to yourself. You may find it helpful to add your own personal coping statements to the list. Some people find it useful to keep a "cope card" in their wallet with a list of their top ten coping statements. Try these:

I know I am feeling anxious right now; let's see what I can do about it.

One step at a time. I can handle this situation.

It's overwhelming right now, but I will choose one thing to work on for now.

I will make a safety plan.

This anxiety is normal; now what can I do about it?

This is a reminder to use my coping exercises.

Relax. I'm in control. Take a slow, deep breath.

What have I done in the past to successfully deal with this?

I've gotten through this kind of thing before.

It will be over shortly. It will feel much better in a few moments.

It's not the worst thing that can happen.

Describe what is around you. That way you won't think about worrying.

Keep focusing on the present: what is it I have to do?

I won't try to eliminate my fear totally, just keep it manageable.

I can reason my fear away. I have a few ways I can do this.

Let me just close my eyes and relax for a second.

NEGATIVE AFFIRMATIONS

You don't often hear psychologists talk about negative affirmations, but gently accepting some harsh realities may be a way of healing and thinking rationally. Some examples:

He will not change. I have to accept that.

Narcissists do not show healthy love and affection.

There is no use waiting for her to get better. It will not happen.

The narcissist targeted me for my good qualities.

Marital therapy may be counterproductive with a narcissist.

I have to accept that there will be no closure here.

BREATHING AND MINDFULNESS

The next several items are part of a comprehensive program of relaxation. The first step is to learn to use paced breathing techniques. This is just another way to distract you from the usual stressful ideas (like "What do I have to do tomorrow?" or "I should have accomplished more today"). Focusing should be done while you are visualizing your relaxation scene (see next section). The combination of visualization and focusing will help you disregard stress-producing thoughts and allow you to relax physically and emotionally, at least for a little while.

When we are anxious or stressful, our breathing becomes shallow and irregular. Practice keeping your breathing evenly paced. Concentrate on each breath as you breathe in and out. Choose a neutral word to focus on while practicing relaxation and visualization. The words *one*, *calm*, and *relax* work well. Each time you breathe out, say one of these words to yourself. This will assist in keeping your breathing evenly paced and help reduce the chance of stressful thoughts intruding.

Say the word *one* with each exhale throughout the next few relaxation exercises.

Mindfulness techniques train you to be "in the moment," disregarding, for the time being, worries about the future or ruminations about the past. This is what baby boomers used to refer to as being "very Zen." The next time you find your mind racing with stress, try using the acronym S.T.O.P.:

S—Stop what you are doing, put things down for a minute.

T—Take a breath . . .

O—Observe your thoughts, feelings, and emotions . . .

P—Proceed with something that will support you in the moment.

Another popular mindfulness technique is the "countdown," or "five things":

Look for FIVE things you can see: Notice the color of a chair or the shape of a plant; take time to really look around you.

Feel for FOUR things you can touch: The hardness of the chair underneath you, the softness of the shirt you are wearing. Maybe take notice of the sensation of the ground beneath you.

Acknowledge THREE things you can hear: Try not to make judgments, just listen. The breeze blowing through trees, a lawnmower in the distance.

Notice TWO things you can smell: If this feels hard at first, take a big breath in and focus on the lingering scent in the air, or inhale the smell of detergent in the shirt you're wearing.

Become aware of ONE thing you can taste: Bad breath counts; maybe it's the coffee you had that morning or the onions you munched on for lunch.

Repeat this process as many times as necessary to bring yourself back to the present. Take time to notice how you feel afterward. Remember that no matter how far your mind wanders or how elevated you start to feel, the present moment is always there for you to come back to.

VISUALIZE INNER PEACE

Visualization plays an important role in easing tension. Learn to use visualization with a personal relaxation scene. The first step is to create the scene. It can be based on a real experience (such as a vacation you took, a beach you visited, or a walk in the forest), or it can be totally made up. Think back to a place and time where you were almost totally relaxed. Think of a vacation, walking in a forest, tanning at the beach, looking out over a lake, or just sitting in your backyard watching the trees grow. If you choose an event like a vacation, be sure to dig up some photographs to remind yourself of exactly what the scene looked like. Pick one particular scene or event and stick to it. Be as specific and detailed as possible. Real experiences and memories usually work better, but feel free to embellish and fantasize. Try to be alone in your relaxation scene (no narcissists allowed!). Some examples:

> "I am rowing a wooden boat, alone, on a small lake far away from the city. It is the middle of July. I can hear a waterfall in the distance and the gentle splash of the weathered oars entering the water. I look out over the glassy water and notice a lone, graceful bird skimming the surface. The trees are dark green and bent over with the weight of a recent rain. I can smell the leaves on the surrounding forest floor."

> "I'm lying on a beach at sunset. It is the beginning of my summer vacation from school. There isn't a cloud in the sky. The waves break in white splashes against a background of the orange and

pink sky. The warm wind rushes through my hair as I look up at the darkening blue sky."

"I'm walking slowly through the botanical gardens and stopping at each bed of flowers. Looking out across the blooms, I can smell the leaves on the path in front of me—a very earthy, natural fragrance."

Once you have found a specific relaxation scene, use your senses to make the scene more vivid. The idea is to occupy your mind so you are unable to think about anything else (like stress-producing ideas). Take a good "look" at the relaxation scene in your mind. Imagine the colors in the sky. Are there any clouds? What do they look like? Think of the different shades of green in the trees and in the grass. What does the water look like? Think of the details: birds, animals, waves, colors, textures, sizes, and shapes. More visual details will result in better scenes. Don't forget to use your senses of hearing, smell, and touch to imagine the sounds, odors, and physical landscapes in your scene.

The only thing left to do is bring the scene to life. Make it a moving picture, not a snapshot. Make the waves roll, the birds fly, and the clouds slowly change shape. Look around. Take a walk. Pick a flower. Remember that you are trying to give yourself a break.

Practice visualizing your personal relaxation scene for five minutes each day. Try to make the scene as vivid as possible. Do it with your eyes closed, in a comfortable atmosphere, at a time when you will not be interrupted. Soon you will be able to clearly visualize the scene almost any time you feel tense. Don't worry if you have difficulty visualizing at first. The following muscle relaxation techniques will work even if you have trouble visualizing. By the way, if you fall asleep while practicing—it worked!

PHYSICALLY RELAX

Learn and practice progressive muscle relaxation techniques. Of all the advice in this book, this is the most important for controlling anxiety. These techniques are intended to allow you to physically relax. Muscle groups are arranged in opposing pairs of flexors and tensors. For each muscle group, you will alternately tighten and relax one muscle in a pair, and then tighten and relax the other muscle in the pair.

As you do the exercises, you will become familiar with what it feels like for your muscles to be tense and how it feels when they are relaxed. The idea is to become more aware of when your muscles begin to get stiff as a result of stress or anxiety. Eventually, with just a bit of practice, you will be able to relax instantly in stressful situations. You may want to practice for ten minutes just before you go to sleep, and have someone read the instructions to you the first few times. Relaxation, just like good self-care, is a skill—it has to be practiced!

Remember to find a comfortable atmosphere, use a personal relaxation scene, and pace your breathing. All these procedures can be done simultaneously so that you are too occupied to be stressful! Ideally, the tensing and flexing in these exercises should be done to the point of moderate discomfort, but don't push yourself. Previous injuries or other medical conditions may limit your ability to apply stress to certain muscle groups.

Hands

Tense: Clench both of your hands into tight fists. Squeeze as hard as you can. Keep your wrists and arms loose and relaxed. Focus on the sensation of tightness and stiffness in your knuckles, fingertips, and palms. Hold this for about seven seconds.

Relax: Slowly return your hands to a relaxed position. Feel the warmth in your knuckles and the stiffness leaving the back of your hands. As you relax, try to make your visualization particularly vivid.

Flex: Now, spread your fingers out as far as they will go. Spread them out hard. Notice the sensation of your skin stretching between your fingers and across your palms. Your hands should feel tight, stretched out, and uncomfortable. Stay this way for about ten seconds. Think of removing the tension as you relax your hands back to their normal position.

Relax and Focus: Focus on the feeling of relaxation in the muscles of your hands. Notice the contrast between the sensation of tension and the sensation you are now feeling. Pace your breathing, and keep your relaxation scene sharp in your mind.

Arms and Elbows

Tense: Bend your arms in as far as you can (as if "making a muscle"). Keep your shoulders, wrists, and hands relaxed. You should feel the muscles in your upper arm become hard and stiff. Bend as hard as you can and focus on the feeling of tension at your elbows.

Relax: Slowly straighten out your arms. Pay attention to the feeling of warmth as your muscles get soft and tension-free. Count slowly to yourself from one to seven.

Flex: Now, straighten out your arms as tightly and as stiffly as you can. Imagine you are trying to bend your arms backward, against your elbows. You should feel tightness at the back of your arm, as if your arm was one long rod. Hold your arms stiff for about seven seconds, and then slowly relax.

Relax and Focus: Notice how your muscles soften as you relax your arms. They should feel warm and loose. Look at the surroundings in your relaxation scene and try to become even calmer. Say your relaxation word each time you exhale.

Shoulders

Tense: Bend your shoulders forward. Try to get them to meet in front of your chest. Push as hard as you can. Keep your arms, wrists, and neck as relaxed as possible. You should feel tension and stiffness building in your back and at your shoulders. Focus on this feeling of tension. Count to yourself from one to seven.

Relax: Slowly release the tension in your shoulders by bringing them back to a comfortable position. Feel the stiffness leaving your back and neck. Concentrate on the feelings of relaxation in your shoulders and back for seven seconds.

Flex: Now stick your chest out all the way and push your shoulders together behind your back. You should feel tension at your shoulders, near your shoulder blades, and in the middle of your back. Push your shoulders together hard and hold them there for a few seconds. Then slowly relax your shoulders, neck, and upper arms completely.

Relax and Focus: You should feel a general sensation of relaxation and comfort throughout your upper body and shoulders. Center your thoughts on the calmness you are now feeling. This is the feeling that you want to achieve any time you experience stress during the day. As you are relaxing, think of the relaxation scene you have created. Make the "you" in the scene even more relaxed than before. Keep your breathing paced, and say your relaxation word as you exhale.

Mouth and Jaw

Tense: Clench your teeth as hard as you can. Bite down until you feel tightness in your jaw and stiffness in the muscles on the lower part of your cheeks. Your jaw should feel tight and hard. Focus on this feeling of tightness for about seven seconds.

Relax: Relax your jaw completely. Keep your teeth slightly apart, lips loosely together. Concentrate on the relief and relaxation you are experiencing in your jaw muscles.

Flex: Open your mouth and keep it open as wide as you possibly can. Imagine opening your mouth to bite a very large apple. You can feel a definite stiffness in your jaw and perhaps a ringing in your ears. The muscles of your jaw feel hard and sore. After about seven seconds, slowly close your mouth.

Relax and Focus: Concentrate and focus on the feeling of relaxation in the muscles you have just tensed. It should feel particularly good to relax these muscles. Focus on the sensation of relaxation and softness in your face, neck, shoulders, and arms. Try to imagine yourself becoming even more relaxed than you are now. Concentrate only on the feelings in your face, eyes, forehead, and mouth as you say your relaxation word, and keep your relaxation scene vivid in your mind.

Don't put pressure on yourself to relax perfectly. Relaxation is a skill that has to be learned and practiced. If you find yourself to be somewhat nervous or tense during these exercises, don't worry—just remain as relaxed as possible. If unpleasant or anxious thoughts enter your mind, just try to push them out as much as possible for now. The first few times you practice relaxing, your goal should be to feel just a little more relaxed than when you started. You will feel more and more relaxed with practice.

TAKE CARE OF YOURSELF

Stay healthy. Try to maintain good nutrition, even when you are rushed and busy. Try eating smaller meals more often during the day. This will keep your blood sugar level consistent and prevent anxiety. Take dietary supplements, such as vitamins, if you don't eat right. Get a reasonable amount of exercise (walking, aerobics, bowling, golf, even window shopping) and stay current with medical checkups. Get enough sleep, and try to keep your sleeping patterns regular. As a general rule, stay away from foods containing caffeine (coffee, tea, cola, chocolate, certain cakes and cookies), especially after four p.m. Physical well-being is directly related to emotional health.

REWARD YOURSELF! YOU DESERVE IT

Give yourself reinforcement after you have successfully tried any of the techniques described above, even if the outcome was not exactly what you wanted. Relaxation is a skill that needs to be practiced. It is very important to be self-rewarding. It encourages you to try again and protects you from being overwhelmed by situations out of your control. Rewards do not have to be monetary. Try listening to a favorite CD, playing a game, taking a long private bath, or calling a long-distance friend. Get in the habit of self-rewarding every accomplishment, major or minor.

A few more important notes about self-care: As you develop a consistent and meaningful self-care routine, and as you grow and mature as a person recovering from an abusive relationship, your friends and family members may not grow with you. You will disappoint some people when you prioritize yourself. You need to care for yourself first at this time.

Sometimes self-care means doing things that you do not feel like doing. Exercising, making tough decisions, and pushing yourself in a new direction can be challenging. Your newly reinforced boundaries may push some people away. Let them go. Self-care does require letting go of some relationships, habits, and choices that are comfortable but no longer serve you. Self-care is often most difficult just when you need it the most. Don't give up, because the outcome is worth it.

DR. FRED

I am blessed and cursed with a lot of hobbies and interests. Although it is difficult, I try my best to make time for reading, photography, recording amateur music, drawing, writing, and hiking. Anything creative or productive. I immerse myself in my group private practice. And I probably buy too many things on Amazon!

DR. ROBIN

I love to exercise. Some people do it to stay in shape, but I do it mostly to clear my mind (but keeping fit has been a good perk!). There is nothing like a great run or a long walk on a beautiful day. I find that I need some alone time to recoup my energy. I learned this as a result of my own healing after being with the narcissist. When you become grounded in who you are, you really enjoy time alone. I also love being with family and friends, and traveling.

11

Making the Break

STEP 5. PREPARING TO MAKE A MOVE: DIVORCING A NARCISSIST

Safety first! Inform as many trusted friends and family as possible, at least the ones not already corrupted by the narcissist. Make at least one other person aware of your intentions. Don't do anything that may cause an abusive reaction if you can avoid it. The narcissist *will* go into a rage when he or she realizes that you seriously intend to leave. The narcissist *will* go through multiple attorneys until he or she finds one, probably one also in tune with narcissism, who will take and champion their cause. Here is a safety-first checklist:

Change all passwords (bank, apps, emails, social media).

Block the narcissist on all social media platforms.

Lawyer up as soon as possible for legal guidance.

Inform as many friends and family as possible of your intentions and whereabouts.

Don't tell the narcissist what you intend to do until it's absolutely necessary.

Protect money, personal assets, and possessions by moving them to a safe place.

Keep detailed records of everything the narcissist does.

Be ready for narcissistic rage, and stay calm; do not confront or engage.

Do not hesitate to call the police in the event of any danger whatsoever.

Preparation is the key to separating from a narcissist. Get yourself ready and stay organized. Keep records of every transgression and the time and place they occurred. Consult a good, recommended attorney concerning the legality of recording audio and video, moving savings out of an account, or confiscating things belonging to the narcissist.

Change every password you can think of to protect your privacy: bank accounts, social media, safes or lockboxes you have in the house. Block the narcissist on all forms of social media. Eventually, all communication should be through attorneys.

If this sounds like preparation for war, it is. The narcissist will do everything in his or her power to destroy you, at least emotionally. He or she will suddenly find the funding for a top attorney, wipe out bank accounts, contact friends and enemies, launch a smear campaign, accuse you of abuse and narcissism (this is a guarantee), and use everything you have ever said against you. The narcissist will lie about changing himself or herself, promise you anything, and probably suggest marriage counseling. Don't fall for it. It's only a strategy to get your guard down.

AFTER THE SEPARATION OR DIVORCE

Just when you think the narcissistic nightmare is over, you realize that the narcissist remains in your life. He or she will stalk you on social media, continue to contact your friends and family, and continue attempting to make you feel guilty. He or she will bring false legal claims, default on legal agreements, flaunt the new source (partner), and simultaneously try to hoover you back into his or her life. If you have children, the narcissist will not hesitate to use them against you by trying to alienate them from you. He or she will purposely establish conflicting household rules and cause general chaos. The children are *not* the narcissist's main concern.

If you share children with a narcissist, you will still have to communicate some types of information. Try to focus only on necessary communications: school schedules, when to pick up the children for visitation, only essential contact information. Ideally, communication should be made through a third party or attorney if the narcissist is causing drama.

Coparenting with a narcissist is impossible. How do you manage the inevitable conflict with someone whose only goal is to punish *you*? What is one piece of advice to give to someone who is parenting along with a narcissist?

Here are a variety of answers from people who have been there:

Thomas: "When you're parenting with a narcissist, it's hideous, but you have to be the best parent you can be. You are not 'coparenting,' you are mostly counteracting the effects of the narcissist's distorted view of parenting. You have to be a shining example of logic and rationality and calmness, dealing with things in a reasonable way. It's okay if you're the good parent. Eventually, the children see who is manipulating whom, when they are grown enough! All you can do is assert yourself and set boundaries, which the narcissist will continue to try to cross. I live this every day. It's not easy, but you have to train yourself not to respond, not to react, not to get emotional."

Michael: "The toxicity they come with! I tried but I failed, it's been two years. Whenever I tried to talk about my son, she would bring our past in. Then we'd end up not discussing the child."

Francine: "Trying to coparent effectively with my ex is a relentless and thankless endeavor. My number one tip: always have the perspective you approach be from the children's level or point of view. Use clear logic, be rational when speaking to the narcissist, and be consistent in disciplining your children. I call it "business mode" when I give my narcissistic ex basic information about the kids. Filter out the narcissist's usual attempts to engage you emotionally."

Stephanie: "Well, I haven't quite figured it out. He ended up with sole custody from lies, deceit, and manipulation. I tried to talk to him when there was an issue, like the time my son slapped me; he just asked what I did to cause it. My son is, though, waking up . . . He says things about my ex that are right on target."

John: "It's impossible. They either get everything they want or they throw angry tantrums. They lie, and gaslight, and abuse. I have to block her three times a year and resist the urge to respond to her vicious insanity."

Georgette: "You can't coparent. You are parallel parenting and doing damage control. The narcissistic ways will never ever stop . . . My only advice is never trust them, never expect anything good from them, don't enter an emotional argument, disengage from them as much as possible."

Susan: "I had to set very clear boundaries and stick to them. I told my ex he was only allowed to speak with me about the kids. If he started blaming me or deviating from the kids, I would hang up on him, and I have numerous times. I give him the very bare minimum."

Pam: "You document, document, document! Eventually you'll end up in court, 'cause the narcissist will take you there, and then you will go through hell and walk out in victory 'cause you'll have all the proof and they will have nothing to support their idiotic behavior."

Lucy: "Just keep being the good parent you are. Never talk down about the other parent to your children. Always let them love and be with the other parent. It's not your job to make them hate them. Trust your kids."

Paul: "They don't coparent, they counterparent. Follow any court-ordered visitation schedule, and make a file for your records on the narc should they present any problems in writing or phone messages you can file as evidence and use in any police reports."

Bill Eddy, who is both a mental health professional and an attorney, refers to narcissists and other toxic partners as "high-conflict person-alities" (HCPs). HCPs have a recurring pattern of aggressive behavior that increases conflict, especially in the legal realm. These people have an all-or-nothing, black-and-white attitude, uncontrolled emotions, and extreme behavioral outbursts, and they are preoccupied with blaming others. In several of his books, Eddy suggests a kind of expanded gray rock technique he calls the "BIFF response." Any communication with the narcissist in a legal situation, especially written responses, should be Brief, Informative, Friendly, and Firm. Although it's difficult to maintain (especially the friendly part!), this approach can be helpful in a courtroom. The BIFF response may placate the narcissist temporarily, and will assist in legal disputes by demonstrating to the judge that you are reasonable and "not the crazy one." When in family court you should maintain your composure, behave rationally, and stay organized with facts and evidence—even if you are infuriated on the inside. Here's an example:

"I appreciate my ex-wife's generous offer to pick my daughter up one hour earlier than usual on Friday morning, but she has a lot of homework on Thursday nights, so it would make more sense for her to get the usual amount of sleep. My daughter functions much better with a full eight hours."

Brief, unemotional, and to the point

Informative, specific, citing two reasons not to change the pickup time

Friendly, polite, and appreciative

Firm: states the facts and repeats the rationale

We wish there were easier answers to this particular nightmare, but divorcing a narcissist and dealing with coparenting is tough. You have to stay strong, seek emotional support, organize everything, and be very patient. Most of all, be safe. It's essential to join a support group. Neither of the authors could have survived without using social and professional support.

QUESTION: What were the most important things you did to prepare for leaving the narcissist?

DR. FRED

Although I did fear some kind of terrible retaliation from the narcissist, I knew a divorce was inevitable. I consulted a couple of attorneys and chose one with some experience with narcissism (I wasn't happy with her, regardless). I tried to put aside some money. I informed friends about what was going on. I made a plan to pack up my belongings on days when my narcissist was at work. I spent a few days away visiting family in Florida. Even though it was legally ill-advised, I left the house and found my own space to live before the divorce was finalized. This was for my own mental health and emotional survival. I found it important not to worry about small financial matters. The most important thing for me was to get out, get away, and move on. This is not always possible if couples have children together, or joint business ventures, or shared property. In that way, I was fortunate. I did not have any children with the narcissist.

DR. ROBIN

The narcissist's insidious covert abuse over time was so foreign to me, went against my own value system, and contradicted what I thought about relationships and love. I knew that I had to leave the relationship the second the narcissist staged a trivial argument and stayed out all night.

My exit strategy began with setting goals and doing the following: I educated myself on how narcissists think and the cycle of emotional abuse. I also learned about how my codependent thinking contributed to the dysfunctional relationship with the narcissist. I then put my energy into finding the support of friends and family, getting myself organized, and eventually moving out. I was very careful that the narcissist didn't know my plan or anything that I was thinking. Many of us become excellent actors once we are on to the narcissist and decide to exit the relationship.

12

Building New Relationships

STEP 6. HEALTHY RELATIONSHIPS

After a breakup with a narcissist, you will become an expert at spotting other narcissists in your life. It may seem at times that everyone is a narcissist! However, the world is full of "normal," kind, and positive individuals, and it is possible to recognize them and to embrace healthy relationships as your social world expands. Among other things, the following are essential for a long-term, meaningful, and satisfying relationship:

Awareness of the partner's goals, aspirations, plans, and preferences

Ability to allow the partner to influence (not control) you, and respecting their viewpoints

Ability to meaningfully resolve conflicts that are able to be settled

Recognizing and accepting the unresolvable problems in the relationship

Creating a shared meaning as you navigate through life together

Obvious respect, fondness, and friendship between partners

A strong sense of being a couple, of being "on the same team"

A sense of direction in the relationship, even if moving slowly

Significantly more positive communication than negative

Plenty of shared goals, values, and ideas

Not surprisingly, narcissists are not capable of any of these things. Based on John Gottman's well-regarded research about what makes a good, lasting relationship, it is impossible to have a successful marriage with a narcissist. Gottman described four things that ruin a relationship, which he aptly called the Four Horsemen of the Apocalypse:

Criticism: Finding fault, using insults, finding weaknesses

Contempt: Rolling eyes, mocking opinions, smirking

Defensiveness: Avoiding responsibility and blame

Stonewalling: Refusing to discuss, silent treatment, avoiding resolution

These, of course, are the hallmarks of a narcissist. Healthy people in enriching relationships are accountable for their feelings and their actions. They "own" them and are not afraid to admit to their part in difficult situations and conflict. There is a simple clarity with healthy people and relationships. They easily accept responsibility and strive toward resolution of disagreements. Telling the truth is usually effortless.

Healthy people are able to ask for what they need in a relationship and can point out when they are not getting it. This leads to some level of productive discussion and deepens understanding. Asking a narcissist for anything, especially to understand your feelings, is likely to be futile. They can only give when there's something in it for them.

Emotionally mature people apologize and report that it feels good doing it. There is a satisfaction in taking part in the truth. Telling the truth and taking responsibility contribute to healthy relationships.

Healthy people are compassionate. If you make a mistake, so what? People make mistakes. You are human and it is okay to make a mistake, and if you are accountable for your mistake, all the better. Your accountability is a sign of your maturity. A healthy person might gently, kindly, and compassionately encourage you to be accountable, but will likely let it go if you push back. Emotionally healthy people allow you to be you. You are accepted for who you are, faults and all.

Healthy people, unlike narcissists, can disagree. They can put together information that supports their point of view or that aims at the truth without feeling personally threatened. Winning an argument and being right might have tangential value to a healthy person, but to a narcissist, they are everything. Conflict is somehow a demonstration of their personal value, validation of their self-worth. Healthy people can be wrong and get over it. Narcissists can't get over it because, they claim, they are never wrong. The narcissist may even use a disagreement to segue into an argument or diatribe about your flaws. When you debate a narcissist, watch out! They don't play, or argue, fairly.

Support is a foreign concept to the narcissist. When we grow up in a healthy environment, we are taught to have, pursue, and be proud of accomplishing our goals. To a narcissist, our goals detract from attention that ought to be paid to them. Our accomplishments are threats. Consequently, we will likely find ourselves unsupported by the narcissist. Narcissists are not loyal to their partners. They are loyal to themselves and believe that loyalty to them is the only reasonable loyalty. They will deny that our goals are worthy, and any evidence of our progress toward our goals is derided. Their goals are more important than ours. Emotionally healthy people are fully capable of lending support to others' goals, aspirations, hobbies, and pursuits.

As former targets of narcissists, we are in a unique position to recognize emotional dysfunction. After leaving the narcissist and either beginning a new relationship or simply being open to one, we can train ourselves to see telltale traits. Once we are aware of these traits from our previous relationship, we can be on alert for the potential in future partners and avoid those people. We also have to balance hypervigilance with healthy discrimination and caution.

In an article titled "Dating After a Breakup" from The Gottman Institute (gottman.com), Stacy Hubbard, LMFT, offers suggestions for returning to the dating world after leaving a relationship. The longer the relationship, the bigger the challenges will probably be in returning to the dating experience. Letting friends know you are starting to date again can give you some built-in support and people to talk to. It is great to have people we trust whom we can talk to and use as sounding boards.

MANAGING EXPECTATIONS

Not every date is going to be "the one." A date can be a getting-to-know-you experience, a shared cup of coffee with no pressure for the relationship to go anywhere—which, ironically, may make "going somewhere" easier. But there need not be pressure to push the relationship into deeper waters.

REAL PEOPLE, NOT DIGITAL AVATARS

A relationship, even if merely a friendship, stands a better chance of survival if it occurs in person rather than online. Long online interaction ought to be avoided, says Helen Fisher, a consultant for the dating website Match (match.com). Limited text, email, and telephone conversations will let you know if you want to meet and, perhaps, date. When you do, meet in public and someplace safe. Ask open-ended questions, such as what kind of work do you do, how was your day, and what are your hobbies. Don't talk about previous relationships, and, if asked, keep those answers brief. Saying the relationship was painful but that you've gotten past it is perfectly okay.

HOW TO JUDGE THE EXPERIENCE

We have an emotional reaction to a new person in our life. We may feel that spark of attraction or we may not; however, being attracted to a person does not mean we can trust that person. Trustworthy people don't try to dominate the conversation. They allow you to be you, every bit their equal. Trustworthy people are consistent rather than mercurial and ever-changing. They are compassionate and able to see points of view other than their own. They can admit they are wrong and can work with you toward growing the relationship. Safe people can allow the relationship to grow naturally rather than controlling or rushing the progress. They respect your boundaries and have no need to judge others or gossip.

Safe and trustworthy people have no reason to lie, and they will rarely, if ever, engage in unethical or immoral behavior. Leaving a relationship with a narcissist can leave you vulnerable to narcissistic, pathological, or toxic behavior—or your own early life experiences may have left you vulnerable to the narcissist to begin with. If your new relationship seems too much like your old narcissistic one, consider speaking to a professional with experience in this area to examine why you might be drawn to people who are unhealthy for you.

Relearn that a relationship can be fun. Do things you enjoy; find things you can enjoy together. You don't have to immediately gravitate to your new friend or partner's choices, but you can dip your toe in the water and practice your relationship skills by navigating to common ground.

Consider what you are looking for in a relationship. Is it a great date? A night of fun? A long-term relationship? A life partner?

More than half of all marriages end in divorce, and those who navigate challenging issues together successfully tend to succeed better in their relationships over the long term. According to Preston Ni, writing in *Psychology Today*, the single most important criterion for long-term relationship happiness is mutual trust. The degree to which trust was a challenging issue early in life can have an impact on one's ability to trust later on. The dependability of our partners is a good indicator of trust, more so than individual broken promises or agreements. Couples might consider the degree to which each partner values the physical, intellectual, and emotional aspects of the relationship and the degree to which each perceives that the couple shares quality time and activities.

The single strongest negative predictor in relationships is contempt—the degree of criticism, scorn, sarcasm, and negative judgment partners have for one another. When there is disagreement, are the issues personalized and the individual labeled? Or are the issues separate from the perceived innate qualities of each partner? Can you avoid judging the person while focusing on the issue?

Does each partner see the other's communication style as lifting them up or putting them down? If there are communication challenges, do both parties have the willingness to find common ground? How are your conflict resolution skills? Do either of you often find yourselves in "fight, flight, or freeze" mode? Can you resolve your conflicts without harboring ongoing ill will? Do you believe that your disagreements and their resolution lead to growth? Is the relationship getting better over time? Do external crises and emergencies bring you together or drive a wedge between you? Enduring challenging times together often leads to significant strength in the relationship's long-term bonds.

How do your financial values compare? Couples often argue about money, and if they do, the stability of the relationship may be in jeopardy. How do you know if your financial values are compatible? Who paid for the first date? The second? Were there conflicts over these issues? Are nonmonetary gifts appreciated? According to the National Marriage Project, couples who reported disagreeing about finances once a week or more were over 30 percent more likely to eventually divorce than couples who reported disagreeing about finances a few times per year.

How does each of you view the other's financial values? Do you each believe the other seems satisfied with their possessions or that they are frequently seeking to acquire more (higher-end cars, clothing, jewelry, shoes, etc.)? Do you share the same long-term financial goals and agree about the road to achieving them? While it is not reasonable to expect our partners to share *all* our values and goals, finding ways to navigate these issues without increased conflict can be a great indicator of ongoing compatibility.

Research at the University of California, Davis, has shown that in their early stages, long- and short-term relationships often appear nearly identical. But their trajectories begin to diverge after weeks or months. Paul Eastwick, the lead author of a UC Davis study differentiating the qualities of long- and short-term relationships, surveyed more than eight hundred people of varying ages and asked them to note the quality of the relationship from its inception, in some cases even before the dating phase. Eastwick noted that little data exists on the period in relationships after couples meet but prior to sexual contact. The study found that romantic interest arises at similar rates in long- and short-term relationships, but that it peaks and begins to wane more quickly in short-term relationships; in long-term relationships it peaks at a significantly later point. Typically, the point at which the two trajectories begin to diverge is about the point at which the relationship becomes sexual. In other words, people usually know after having their initial sexual experiences with their partner whether they want the relationship to grow into something more. Couples may continue to have sexual encounters while attracted to one another to some degree, but relationships will tend to last longer when time spent together is found to be exciting and meaningful, when values are shared, and when the happiness of one's partner is important. These differences become apparent soon after sexual contact.

Readers of Buzzfeed were asked to offer their insights on long-term relationships. Following are some highlights of their experiences and suggestions.

1. Relationships constantly change, and being open to that change and embracing it leads to stability. Loving and accepting one another for who you are rather than trying to change one another is another criterion for success. We can always be working on ourselves, and allowing our partner to do the same bodes well for the relationship.

2. Fan the flames of flirtation and romance, no matter how long you are together. Going to bed while angry can lead to waking up angry the next day. Better to solve the disagreement and make up. Interestingly, other respondents said exactly the opposite. Don't try to make up while you're still mad. Sleeping on it may give you time and space to cool down. You may be more apt to see the other person's point of view when you are calmer. Apologize, even if you think you're right. Expressing regret can bring you together, and chances are you may regret something you said or the way you said it. Ultimately, it is up to you and your partner to decide which style and timing of conflict resolution is best for you.

3. Make sure to communicate about everything. Don't make the assumption that your partner knows what you are

thinking. They are not mind readers! And when you do communicate, do so courteously and politely. Whatever they say back, listen! Your partner really is doing his or her best to tell you what they are feeling. They deserve to be heard, just as you deserve to be heard. It's also a matter of trust, difficult after a narcissistic experience.

4. Comparing your partner to someone else isn't fair. We are not privy to other people's complete versions of themselves, whereas we see our partners at their best and worst. What we see of most people is what they allow us to see on social media or in public, so comparisons to people we may have a more complete picture of are not fair. Instead, take a clear look at your partner, keeping in mind the challenges he or she has to deal with. Life isn't easy, for anyone.

5. Relationships have ebbs and flows. Each of you will have your good and not-so-good days when each will be stronger and more adaptable or more vulnerable. That's okay. Relationships work best when you allow one another your good and not-so-good days, remembering that you are both human and fallible. Love their fallibility and they will love yours!

6. Do "sweat the small stuff." If you resolve differences while they are still small, they won't have time to grow into mountains. Consider the "rule of five." Will the issue you are struggling with matter in five minutes, five days, five weeks, five months, or five years? Time heals pretty much all wounds and will keep others from getting worse. Keep your differences in perspective; don't nurse grudges or harbor hurts.

Learning to Trust Again

Having the willingness to allow yourself a new relationship is a courageous step. If your little narcissist was a significant other, then trusting another person was a source of pain. How do you enter into another love relationship? How do you trust? How can you allow yourself to be vulnerable? By being careful. By taking baby steps. You can spend time with someone new without allowing the relationship to grow into something more significant emotionally and/or sexually, at least for a while. You can enjoy one another's company, and as you do, you will get a sense of your new friend's emotional honesty. You want to protect yourself from ever being subjected to narcissistic abuse again. Well, you are now an expert in the field, from the perspective of having been an unwilling participant. You know what a narcissistic relationship looks and feels like, from the inside. You can go slowly, with your antennae up, and be on the lookout for the sort of manipulative narcissistic signposts you know so well. Be careful, but also be aware that healthy, caring relationships are possible, and that is exactly what you deserve, when the time is right for you.

Is Your New Relationship in Balance?

A relationship can be considered a combination of commitment, intimacy, and passion. Think of these qualities as three sides of a triangle. Very few relationships make a perfect triangle, but if yours is way out of line you may be feeling frustrated, angry, or resentful. Find the shortest side of your "love triangle" and focus on improving things in that area first. Use the definitions below as a guide.

Commitment is how dedicated you are to keeping your relationship alive and healthy, or how true you are to your partner. Here are some synonyms: fidelity, responsibility, obligation, duty, seeing things through. Commitment in a relationship means that most obstacles can be overcome, and there is a willingness to be faithful even in bad times. How would you rate your level of commitment?

Intimacy is the closeness in a relationship, the things you share with your partner that nobody else knows, the secrets and the common experiences. Intimacy is much more than sexual tenderness and physical closeness; it's how comfortable you are being with your partner. Can you express yourself openly without fear of criticism? Do you feel heard when you are speaking? Can you be vulnerable without getting hurt? Intimacy in a relationship is what makes you friends and makes you feel that each other's presence is familiar and comfortable. How would you rate the level of intimacy in your relationship?

Passion is the immediacy of a relationship. Do you rush home because you can't wait to see your partner? Do you value the weekends together because you know you'll be able to talk to your partner and spend uninterrupted time together? Is time with your partner the highlight of your day? Passion contributes to the spontaneity in your relationship. The creativity, drive, desire, and attraction.

Nothing is perfect, but most healthy relationships have a balance of commitment, intimacy, and passion. If things are off-balance in these areas, relationships can feel like one-night stands or be unfulfilling or disappointing in other ways.

Maintaining a Healthy Relationship

When you find a great new partner, and you are in an emotionally healthy relationship, here are twelve things you can do to keep it that way:

1. Always make time to talk about how your day went. Even ten or fifteen minutes spent in conversation can help the two of you stay in touch and feel closer. Schedule this time together and take turns relating some of the events of the day. Try to choose a time that is not extremely hectic. You may have to practice just listening to your partner, especially if you both have had very busy days.

2. Understand that there *is* such a thing as a good argument. As long as honest feelings were expressed and eventually understood, and as long as there was some conclusion where both partners believed that something was accomplished, then you had a successful argument. Extremely abusive language, sustained hostility, and open threats are *not* part of a good argument.

3. Don't forget to maintain the little niceties, such as saying "please" and "thank you" and generally showing respect and recognition for everyday courtesies. As relationships mature, simple things become more important. Give small, thoughtful gifts and cards even when there is no occasion. Take time out to show your partner how much you appreciate the everyday things they do. The little things are most likely what attracted your partner to you in the first place.

4. Never rely on your partner (or anyone else) to make you happy. Only you can do that. Have your own hobbies, interests, pastimes, and activities separate from those of your partner. Although it is a goal of a healthy relationship to enjoy things together, doing everything together can result in boredom, resentment, and feeling trapped. If you get satisfaction from your daily activities, you will be more relaxed and content when spending time with your partner.

5. Do not assume that your partner will automatically know what your feelings, needs, wants, and preferences are, or what mood you are in. Of course, don't assume you know what your partner is really thinking or feeling. Don't rely on ESP. Even close partners are not mind readers. If you want to know what your partner is thinking, just ask. If you want your partner to know how you feel, tell them.

Take what your partner says at face value, and stop second-guessing.

6. Sexually, learn how to ask for what you want. Again, don't assume your partner has ESP or psychic powers. A little bit of talking while being affectionate will help your partner understand your preferences. Don't be afraid to ask for and give feedback. Learn how to listen.

7. Learn how to accept the natural ups and downs of a relationship. Nothing is perfect, and love will always be accompanied by a certain amount of hurt, tension, frustration, misunderstanding, and jealousy. If your relationship is mostly healthy, with a reasonable amount of communication and a minimum amount of anger and resentment, and if you continue to find that you and the relationship are growing for the better, you have very little to worry about. It's those people who never argue that make us suspicious!

8. In a healthy relationship, both partners are continually growing and improving. Healthy relationships should bring out the best in each partner. They should inspire, motivate, and enhance one's creativity and well-being. If you are waiting for your partner to change or actively attempting to make them into something they are not, you may be very disappointed. Individual personality, habits, and general style are not likely to change very much. What you see is what you get!

9. Every relationship can benefit from a periodic change of pace. Try a new restaurant. Take a trip to a nearby location chosen at random. Rent a hotel room even if you have privacy at home. Another idea is to experiment with fantasy. Try a style of clothing that you have never worn. Learn how to be playfully unpredictable. Creativity will

keep a relationship fresh. For a sense of romance, try looking at old photographs of you and your partner, or read cards and letters that you have sent to each other. It can also be fun to recount what your first few dates were like.

10. Recognize some of the differences between men and women. Men: Women typically enjoy conversation, conversing in groups, and expressing detail verbally. They tend to dream in detail, interpret situations in terms of personal motives, feelings, and consequences, and appreciate positive feedback for personal accomplishments. Women like to hear words of support and understanding, not advice, suggestions, or harsh criticism. Women: Men tend to enjoy variety, respond well to good-natured challenges, and place a high value on personal space and privacy. In social situations, men are more likely to interpret events at face value. If men display an emotional side, give positive reinforcement. Stereotypes can be dangerous, but recognizing real differences is vital for good communication.

11. Give yourself reinforcement after you have successfully tried one of the techniques to improve your relationship, even if the outcome was not exactly what you wanted. It is very important to be self-rewarding. Both you and your partner should reward yourselves for working together. Try listening to a favorite song together, finding a new song to share, playing a game, or going out to a movie or for some special dessert.

12. Avoid knots in communication or recurring circular arguments that keep going nowhere without ever getting resolved. These snarls of circular logic seem like endless loops and can take on a life of their own. Try to get at the

underlying issues behind these kinds of arguments, and view them as a puzzle for the both of you to solve. Try to think of disagreements as opportunities to improve or understand your partner better. Though it's difficult to develop, this attitude will make almost any argument easier to resolve.

QUESTION: What are the most important signs that you are in a healthy relationship?

DR. FRED

For me, the most tangible sign that I had found a great person and a healthy relationship was calmness. Of course, we had exciting times together, but the general tone of day-to-day life was peace and contentment. Easy communication, very few disagreements, and a shared vision of the future. I had to get used to the romantic gestures being far more genuine but less showy. Our plans together were less grandiose but far more meaningful. After being in a six-year narcissistic relationship, it took me a bit of time to stop anticipating or expecting problems. I'd get a brief knot in my stomach if I was five minutes late coming home from work or forgot to do something. My internal thought was, "Is it okay if I talk to her about this?" In the beginning I felt like Laurence Olivier's character in the movie *The Marathon Man*, constantly asking, "Is it safe?" Although I had felt completely prepared to begin a new relationship, there are always residual effects of exposure to a narcissist.

DR. ROBIN

The most important sign for me is that when we have a disagreement or argument, he cares and does everything he can to make it better. He doesn't just roll over and go to sleep when I've felt upset. Communication and compromise are also important signs of a healthy relationship. You feel comfortable and calm with each other. Drama, triangulating others, and smearing your partner are definitely not parts of the relationship!

13

On the Move

STEP 7. MOVING AWAY, MOVING PAST, MOVING ON

Emerging from a narcissistic relationship is like waking up from a nightmare. Yet while leaving the narcissist in your rearview mirror is a good thing, recovering from the trauma of being in a narcissistic relationship can be challenging and time-consuming. Recovery can require digging deep and finding a qualified professional to help you work through the process and then staying with it.

Learning to be a separate entity from the narcissist is necessary in order to make yourself a priority. Once you do this, the trauma bonds will begin to lift and you will start feeling a little bit better. But it all begins with self-care.

You were trained by the narcissist to become addicted, to become his or her supply. Now you can train yourself to be free of the narcissist by living for yourself, right now in this moment. Thinking this way is a skill that can be honed to a fine point, so you are hyperaware of even the minute details of your activity. For many this degree of focus is not necessary, but for those of us recovering from narcissistic relationships and struggling with intrusive thoughts and/or feelings, this focus can keep unwanted mental imagery at bay. Cooking dinner can become a step-by-step process: now I am gathering supplies from the fridge, freezer, spice rack; now I am cutting vegetables; now I am cooking rice; and so on, right through to the details of eating: chewing, swallowing, and cleaning up afterward. Such mindfulness shuts out the vestiges of the narcissist. There is simply no room for him or her in your mind.

While you are participating in these activities, notice them; be mindfully aware of the fact that you are in an aerobics class, or walking in the woods, or on the street. Notice the book that you're reading or the music you are listening to, and give yourself credit for taking charge of your life! Be aware that you are moving forward, and imagine your little narcissist getting even smaller in your rearview mirror. Each moment that you are engaged in an activity and no longer focused on your little narcissist can be a reference point to look back on with satisfaction.

Find places where you're accepted for being you. Meetup groups are great. List your interests and look into Meetup (meetup.com) or other groups, even virtual ones, built around common interests. Once you start interacting with these folks, you will feel your sense of self-worth improve. That's because these people, assuming you are in a group with nice people, value you. If you are not in a group with nice people, find a different group!

Being your best self will also affect others in your sphere of influence. If you were married to a narcissist and you have children together, being your best mom or dad with them will model mature behavior and help them become their best selves. If you fear their minds are being poisoned by your former narcissist, the fact that you are modeling mature behavior will be noticed!

Treating others with empathy and compassion invites those behaviors from others when they interact with you. Use good judgment and you'll model good judgment. If you're having a hard day, you can absolutely share that, while being careful not to mistreat others. It's okay to have a bad day, and you can teach that to your children and others in your sphere of influence. If you're being authentic, others will notice and respond in kind. A great response to someone you care about who is having a hard time is to express compassion. "Wow, that must be really hard" is a great, supportive response to their difficulties.

Once you have spent a bit of time by and with yourself, or in the company of people who treat you well, give yourself some credit. You deserve it! Now it's time to build on this success and grow your relationship with you!

As discussed in the previous chapter, you may be ready to begin new relationships. When you realize that the new partner you are with is not a narcissist, you will be refreshed and joyful. In a non-narcissistic relationship, you can safely be yourself. It's transformative!

Feeling safe and trusted, as well as feeling comfortable trusting others, will be a milestone. Your new friend or partner will have their own map of their world and the future. Trust means being able to share that at your and their own pace and loving the map and the pace at which it is revealed. This is what authenticity looks like!

This awareness that we are safe in a relationship allows us to be vulnerable, which both strengthens the bonds that hold the relationship together and allows a depth of feeling and exposure to occur naturally, whereas without this awareness of safety, we tend to hold the other person at an emotional arm's length. When we have trust and a deeply felt sense of safety, we are willing to remain devoted to the relationship, to weather the storms that may otherwise pull us apart.

Escaping the narcissist is a journey of personal growth. As we emerge into the light, we can first heal and then expand our lives by discovering what inspires us. There are many good books about identifying and leaving pathological relationships and learning to live more rewarding lives. If we are not ready to engage with others, reading can be a toe in the water, an introductory experience. We can read and quickly see that some of these authors have walked in similar shoes. We can highlight these books and return to them whenever we need them. We can identify and visit online forums—first as observers and perhaps later as participants. This provides an initial way to connect with other people safely.

Finding yourself involved with a psychopath is an adventure, that's for sure. It will open your eyes to human nature, our broken society, and, perhaps most important of all, your own spirit. It's a dark journey that will throw you into spells of depression, rage, and loneliness. It will unravel your deepest insecurities, leaving you with a lingering emptiness that haunts your every breath.

You deserve to be the priority. This will come naturally as you heal, with the help of a professional and by reading and engaging on some level with others. You are in control of your healing, of your future. You get to decide which roads to take to the top of your beautiful, personal mountain.

The post-narcissist emotional landscape is so different from the view from the cycle of abuse you have suffered. Imagine being on a rocky planet with dangerous plant and animal life, a toxic atmosphere, and an oppressive climate. That's the image of the narcissistic, psychopathic landscape. Now imagine being transported to a beautiful mountaintop, with clean air and flowers. Yes, there may be dangers here too, but they're dangers you are aware of and have learned to avoid. This is akin to the post-narcissist landscape. You won't arrive there in a day, but with work and the right mix of inputs, you will get to a beautiful place. You'll see!

Be patient as you begin to emerge from the darkness of narcissistic abuse into the light of self-nurturing, healing, and healthy interactions with others. The painful effects you suffered and the changes you underwent at the hands of your little narcissist did not happen overnight, and the healing and changes needed to become your best self will take some time.

As we learn intuitively to care for ourselves, we notice traits in others that we want in our lives. As we learn to engage with others in safe, even nurturing, ways, we find ourselves out of the fog and increasingly engaged with life. We are more creative, we have more energy—our life force is enlivened. We begin to be delighted with our encounters with people and with nature as we fill our life with joy and happiness.

QUESTION: Can you describe any positive experiences or effects as a result of having known the narcissist?

DR. FRED

Dr. Robin and I have discussed this many times. I would never want anyone to suffer the horrors of being in a relationship with a narcissistic abuser. However, the experience has had quite a few positive effects. After learning so much about narcissism and, in the process, about myself, I can almost say I'm glad that it happened. I am so much stronger, more aware of who I am, more conscious of what I want and what I need, and more attuned to others in similar situations. I am, obviously, much more alert when it comes to people who do not contribute to my well-being, and so I no longer waste my time dealing with narcissists in any realm. The capacity to help others now has been a gift. I have noticed that across social media nobody is more willing to help someone suffering from narcissistic abuse than someone who has been there. I am pleased to be counted among that community.

DR. ROBIN

This is a spiritual journey, and I'm so fortunate that this occurred in my life. I have an incredible community of other thrivers that I'm blessed to be part of. Not only did I heal childhood wounds and address my codependency issues, but I'm also able to pay it forward and help others on their journey. When I first meet a patient who is distraught and trying to leave their emotionally abusive relationship, I look at them and tell them, "I've got you, I've been there, and you too will heal and thrive . . . I promise."

TO FORGIVE OR NOT TO FORGIVE?

A ubiquitous question that we get during our live broadcasts is, "Should I forgive the narcissist?" Often this is associated with understanding that the narcissist is damaged and may have gone through their own hell as a child. Sometimes the question is based on religious beliefs. Although the narcissist is far less innocent and far more intentional and deliberate than you might think, are they deserving of forgiveness regardless?

One thing is certain: if you forgive the narcissist for the damage they have caused, you are doing it for your own emotional and spiritual well-being, not for them. Forgiving is a personal choice, an internal decision. It's a private accommodation and does not have to be anyone else's business. As a reference, and for some perspective, I recommend a book by Simon Wiesenthal called *The Sunflower*.

While imprisoned in a Nazi concentration camp, Wiesenthal was taken from his work detail to the bedside of a dying member of the SS. Haunted by the crimes in which he had participated, the German officer wanted to confess to, and obtain absolution from, a Jew. Faced with the choice between compassion and justice, silence and truth, Wiesenthal said nothing. But even years after the war had ended, he wondered: Had he done the right thing? Did he handle this pivotal moment the way he should have—correctly, morally, spiritually? What would you have done in his place?

In this important book, fifty-three distinguished men and women respond to Wiesenthal's questions. They are theologians, political leaders, writers, jurists, psychiatrists, human rights activists, Holocaust survivors, and victims of attempted genocides in Bosnia, Cambodia, China, and Tibet. Their responses, as varied as their experiences of the world, remind us that Wiesenthal's questions are not limited to events of the past. Here are the results.

Would not forgive the Nazi on his deathbed: 62 percent

Would forgive the Nazi on his deathbed: 19 percent

Could not decide whether or not to forgive: 18 percent

The results may make you think. If almost 20 percent of these respected, educated leaders would forgive a mass murderer, an admitted perpetrator of genocide, where does that leave the ex-partner of a narcissist? One difference is that the Nazi asked for forgiveness. The odds of a narcissist genuinely recognizing what they have done and sincerely requesting forgiveness is very slim. Again, it's a personal decision to forgive, an intimate consideration within yourself. If it gives you a sense of calm and resolve, if it brings peace to your spirit, then forgive. Most important, if it assists you in moving on with your life, then it's the right thing to do. And if you choose never to forgive them, so be it. Not everyone deserves our compassion, and maybe it's not up to us to make that distinction.

14

Share the Joy

STEP 8. GIVING BACK

Now it is time to apply what you have learned and practiced to the rest of your life. Your narcissistic relationship very likely affected many aspects of your life. Exposure to a narcissist will have devastating effects in all of these areas: finances, organization, career, friendships, health, physical activity, spirituality, and creativity. Focusing on improving these eight aspects will help you rebuild your life in a way that will be even better than you thought possible. Once you feel that progress is being made in any of these areas, the most satisfying thing to do is to help others who are still trapped in abusive, narcissistic relationships.

Doing volunteer work and being supportive of others will give you a deep awareness that you are a good person, a perception that a relationship with a narcissist cannot help but damage. Being helpful to others is wonderful evidence to the contrary—you are indeed a good person, and your support of others is proof! In time, you will probably not need this proof, but in the short term, it is a great shortcut to developing a healthy self-image and an ongoing resistance to narcissists.

Having been through this traumatic experience and survived and come out the other side, we have an awareness, a consciousness that can bring us gratitude and motivate us to continue to grow and share. You are now a survivor. You've "been there, done that." You've endured, survived, thrived, and are well along the way to recovery from narcissistic abuse. You are stronger, wiser, more aware, and even a better person for having experienced your horrific ordeal. Please understand that you are in a uniquely qualified position to help others. Do, absolutely, support and comfort others who may be at the beginning of this ordeal.

> **QUESTION:** Do members in the general public know enough about narcissism to keep themselves safe and prevent narcissistic abuse?

DR. FRED

I am very pleased that good, accurate information about narcissistic abuse is more readily available than in the past. Even during the six or seven years that have passed since my own experience there has been a huge proliferation of websites, books, and social media accounts exclusively dedicated to this topic. Not all of the available information is perfect, but the good stuff is out there. It is personally and professionally satisfying to know that I am helping people in uniquely treacherous circumstances. If someone out there feels a little less alone, that's very positive.

DR. ROBIN

Within the past few years, information regarding narcissistic abuse has become widespread. For the most part, we know how to spot a narcissist based on their behaviors. We also know that they can lurk in most any environment (friend groups, home, work) and that we should stay away from them if possible. While it is important that information on narcissistic abuse is becoming mainstream, I'm hopeful that even more education will become readily available regarding how individuals can abstain from entering into an abusive relationship. I believe that this starts with educating preteen children. When narcissistic abuse education becomes mandatory in schools as part of health class curricula, that will make me feel a lot more positive.

15

A Special Message for Therapists (and Clients)

As a whole, psychotherapists are terrible at helping people out of psychopathic, narcissistic relationships. Most of our scientific information on abuse is based on research concerning domestic violence and physical abuse, not specifically the impact on relationships from personality disorders. Also, there are currently very few studies, if any, on male survivors of narcissistic abuse. Psychologists, psychiatrists, social workers, mental health counselors, marriage counselors, and medical professionals who are in a position to help are getting information about a distinctly different population. Although there is a fair amount of overlap, information exclusive to domestic violence may lead to ineffective, or just incorrect, advice for survivors of narcissistic abuse. Just as devastating is the tendency of professionals to apply their own favorite theories of personality to a situation that requires very specific, unique insights and experience. Many professionals are operating on theories learned from one graduate school course on personality disorders.

In regard to providing meaningful information specifically about narcissism, personality disorders in general, and pathological relationships, some therapists are giving potentially harmful advice. Here are some things that therapists should definitely not be doing:

1. Suggesting individual psychotherapy for the narcissistic partner. It does not work. Even with prolonged professional therapy, only a small fraction of individuals with a personality disorder ever improve.

2. Suggesting marital therapy as an option. If the partner has a personality disorder, this will fail. Even worse, it will lead to the victim being "thrown under the bus," sabotaged, and ambushed at the very first session. Marital counseling will most likely do more harm than good. The target of abuse, as a client in the mental health system, may even be shocked and appalled that the well-trained mental health professional is so easily duped by a "professional" narcissist.

3. Suggesting sympathy for the narcissist because he or she had an abusive, neglectful, or otherwise traumatic childhood. The truth is that most individuals with personality disorders did *not* have overly traumatic or adverse childhoods. Their condition is a more complex mixture of genetics, neurology, and deviance. And they are aware of exactly what havoc they wreak.

4. Spending an inordinate amount of time figuring out what is "wrong" with you, including labeling you as codependent or having issues with separation anxiety, neediness, or even masochism. Some of these issues may fit, and if they do, it's essential that they be addressed. But research reveals that for the majority of women leaving narcissistic relationships, these labels are inappropriate. As usual, there is a paucity of information on men in the same situation.

5. Suggesting an arbitrary amount of time that is needed fully to recover before you are ready to move on. Certainly, after a prolonged relationship with a narcissist, time is needed to examine, heal, and "get your head straight"; however, this time period varies greatly from person to person. You may not need as much time as your therapist, or you, initially thought. And you do not need to be one hundred percent healed in order to consider the first steps of moving on.

So that's what therapists shouldn't do. Here are things your therapist definitely *should* be doing:

1. Identifying, emphasizing, and talking directly about the strong possibility that your partner has a personality disorder, is pathological, or is a narcissist. Even if your therapist has never met your abusive partner, they should not hesitate to suggest, based on details of their behavior, that you are dealing with a narcissist.

2. Clearly giving you accurate and current information about personality disorders, such as the following:

    a. Personality disorders are persistent; they do not improve.

    b. The pathological behaviors and thoughts are enduring; they won't go away, fade, or ever stop.

    c. A pathological relationship with a narcissist can be extremely dangerous. It can lead to serious physical, emotional, social, and financial harm.

    d. Personality disorders are mostly not a result of adverse or abusive childhood experiences. The behaviors of a narcissist are not learned, and so they cannot be unlearned. They are not necessarily a result of childhood experiences, not a result of core irrational beliefs, and not a direct result of dysfunctional family issues. They are genetic, innate, inborn, neurological, and deviant. It is not completely incorrect to refer to them as "evil."

e. The narcissist does specifically prowl, identify, hunt, groom, and search for specific "types." You were sought out and targeted.

f. A narcissistic partner is a cyclone of destruction and emotional damage, even if he or she does not meet every criterion for a clinical diagnosis of narcissistic personality disorder. If two or three of the diagnostic criteria are present, that's enough to ruin your life.

Here are additional things therapists should know, specifically about you:

1. The aftereffects of being with a narcissist are not necessarily a result of trauma bonding, Stockholm syndrome, or any disorder on the victim's part. Some therapists can subtly blame you, the victim, by overemphasizing reasons why you got involved with or chose to stick with your toxic partner.

2. Symptoms of post-narcissist exposure are very similar to those of post-traumatic stress disorder or complex PTSD. These symptoms include high levels of anxiety, nightmares, flashbacks, recurring unwanted memories, sleeplessness, inability to concentrate, irritability, loss of focus and concentration, fatigue, and depression.

3. You are most likely experiencing cognitive dissonance about yourself, the narcissist, and the relationship itself. Dissonance refers to the horrible discomfort involved with

maintaining two conflicting thoughts or feelings in your mind at the same time. Therapists must address, identify, treat, and help resolve these internal conflicts concerning the narcissistic relationship. For example:

> The narcissist is a very exciting person—He is also quite sadistic

> She is charming—She is also controlling

> The sex is so amazing—Why am I crying in the bathroom afterward?

> He showers me with affection—He completely ignores me lots of times

> I am well adjusted—But I fell for a psycho!

> I am smart—How could I be so stupid?

> She's so nice to other people—She treats me like shit

> I've never had such excitement!—Why do I feel so horrible inside?

4. You will likely experience flashbacks and obsessive thinking, similar to defining symptoms of PTSD. These are unwanted, intrusive, and very disturbing memories that can be extremely vivid and repetitive. The thing that an untrained therapist may not grasp is that these intrusive memories can be either good or bad. In fact, it's the good memories that can cause the highest degree of cognitive dissonance.

5. Although it can be very helpful and comforting to refer to victims of narcissists as "empaths," the reality is actually far more encouraging and complex. Most victims of

narcissism have elevations in certain nonpathological and very positive traits. These traits, however, lead to difficulties when interacting with a narcissist. Narcissists are well aware that these traits make the survivor vulnerable. The following are some examples of positive traits exploited by narcissists:

- Agreeable
- Trusting
- Humble
- Modest
- Warm and approachable
- Gentle and well-tempered
- Reflective
- Good at finding solutions
- Kind
- Forgiving
- Acts as peacemaker
- Compassionate
- Generous
- Trustworthy
- Optimistic
- Believes people can change
- Responsible
- Capable of enduring
- Tolerant of differing opinions
- Confiding
- Talkative
- Honest
- Altruistic
- Invested in relationships
- Willing to compromise
- Considerate
- Likely to assist, not attack
- Loyal

Faithful	Does not blame others
Committed to obligations	Strong motivation to succeed
Resourceful	Problem solver
Works toward reducing chaos	Does not give up easily
Reliable	Persevering
Feels responsible for outcomes	Diligent

It is painfully obvious why a person with some of the above traits would remain in a dysfunctional relationship and continue trying everything to make it work. It is also woefully apparent why the narcissist is attracted to these personality types: they are ripe and ready to be exploited.

So is it important to find a therapist who has "been there" in terms of actually experiencing narcissistic abuse? Probably. Is it a good idea to seek a therapist who at least has specific and extensive training in personality disorders and the traumatic aftermath of a pathological or narcissistic relationship? Absolutely! Talking to someone who is not familiar with the specific effects of having been abused by someone with a personality disorder can be extremely frustrating, even damaging if the therapist has not been specifically trained in this area.

QUESTION: What is the most important thing you would suggest to someone choosing a mental health professional to help with leaving a narcissist?

DR. FRED

Well, ideally, the therapist should have first-hand experience with having been in a relationship with a narcissist or someone with a similar personality disorder. Hopefully, that therapist will have explored and resolved their own experiences concerning why they were susceptible, how they escaped, and how they recovered. If not personal experience, then the therapist should at least have a deep understanding of personality disorders, the effects they have on others, and the common symptoms, including complex PTSD, that will be seen in the recovery process. If your therapist recommends marital therapy with a narcissist, they are not a qualified therapist. As with finding a good psychotherapist in general, you should be very comfortable during your initial phone call, the therapy process should be carefully explained, and the therapist should be fully credentialed by a recognized licensing board.

DR. ROBIN

Please seek help, as it is extremely difficult to heal on your own. You have been traumatized and retraumatized by the narcissist. I would recommend psychological support in either an individual or group setting. The most important thing to look for in a therapist is that they have been through it themselves and have healed. The therapist should have extensive knowledge regarding trauma, complex PTSD, and cluster B personality disorders.

USEFUL RESOURCES

Akin, Elijah. 2022. "What Is Future Faking and Why Do Narcissists Do It?" *Unfilteredd*, October 5, 2022. https://unfilteredd.net/the-complexity-of-future -faking/.

American Psychiatric Association. 2013. *Diagnostic and Statistical Manual of Mental Disorders*, 5th ed. (DSM-5). Washington, DC: American Psychiatric Association.

Ballard, Zari. 2015. *When Evil Is a Pretty Face: Narcissistic Females and the Pathological Relationship Agenda*. Createspace.

Baum, L. Frank. 1900. *The Wonderful Wizard of Oz* with illustrations by W. W. Denslow. Chicago: George M. Hill.

Bowlby, John. 1969. *Attachment and Loss*. New York: Basic Books.

Brown, Sandra. 2018. *Women Who Love Psychopaths: Inside the Relationships of Inevitable Harm with Psychopaths, Sociopaths and Narcissists,* 3rd ed. Balsam Grove, NC: Sandra Brown.

Brown, Sandra, Claudia Paradise, and William Brennan. 2018. *2-Day Intensive Training on Narcissistic and Psychopathic Abuse*. Workbook. New York: PESI.

Cabaniss, Deborah L. 2019. "Spotting Narcissism: Let Movies Help." *Psychology Today*, August 9, 2019. http://www.psychologytoday.com/us/blog/finding-mind /201908/spotting-narcissism-let-movies-help.

Campbell, Leah. 2021. "33 Ways to Love Yourself More." *PsychCentral*, May 21, 2021. http://www.psychcentral.com/blog/ways-to-love-yourself-more#how-it -works.

Carnegie, Dale. 1936. *How to Win Friends and Influence People*. New York: Simon & Schuster.

Carroll, Lewis. 1866. *Alice's Adventures in Wonderland*, with illustrations by John Tenniel. First US edition. New York: D. Appleton.

Colucci, Lise. n.d. "40 Red-Flag Signs Your Relationship Might Be Toxic." QueenBeeing Narcissistic Abuse Recovery Support. https://queenbeeing.com /40-red-flag-signs-your-relationship-might-be-toxic.

Eddy, Bill. 2008. *High Conflict People in Legal Disputes*. Scottsdale, AZ: HCI Press.

Eddy, Bill. 2008. *It's All Your Fault! Twelve Tips for Managing People Who Blame Others for Everything.* Scottsdale, AZ: HCI Press.

Eddy, Bill. 2011. *BIFF: Quick Responses to High-Conflict People, Their Personal Attacks, Hostile Email and Social Media Meltdowns.* Scottsdale, AZ: Unhooked Books.

Fjelstad, Margalis. 2013. *Stop Caretaking the Borderline or Narcissist: How to End the Drama and Get On with Life.* Lanham, MD: Rowan & Littlefield.

Forward, Susan. 1989. *Toxic Parents: Overcoming Their Hurtful Legacy and Reclaiming Your Life.* New York: Bantam Books.

Frankl, Viktor. 1946. *Man's Search for Meaning.* Boston: Beacon Press.

Gaba, Sherry. 2019. "Trauma Bonding, Codependency, and Narcissistic Abuse." *Psychology Today*, May 29, 2019. http://www.psychologytoday.com/us/blog/addiction-and-recovery/201905/trauma-bonding-codependency-and-narcissistic-abuse.

Garanzini, Salvatore, and Alapaki Yee. n.d. "4 Tips You Need to Know in Your First Year of a Relationship." *The Gottman Institute.* http://www.gottman.com/blog/4-tips-you-need-to-know-in-your-first-year-of-a-relationship.

Gibson, Lindsay. 2015. *Adult Children of Emotionally Immature Parents: How to Heal from Distant, Rejecting, or Self-Involved Parents.* Oakland, CA: New Harbinger.

Gottman, John, and Nan Silver. 2012. *What Makes Love Last? How to Build Trust and Avoid Betrayal.* New York: Simon & Schuster.

Greenberg, Elinor. 2021. "How Narcissists Use Faking to Lure Partners." *Psychology Today*, March 16, 2021. http://www.psychologytoday.com/us/blog/understanding-narcissism/202103/what-is-future-faking-and-why-do-narcissists-do-it.

Hall, Julie. 2017. "4 Insidious Ways Narcissistic Abuse Isolates the Victim." *Narcissist Family Files*, March 23, 2017. http://www.narcissistfamilyfiles.com/2017/03/23/4-insidious-ways-that-narcissistic-abuse-isolates-the-victim.

Hall, Karyn. 2012. "Radical Acceptance." *Psychology Today*, July 8, 2012. http://www.psychologytoday.com/us/blog/pieces-mind/201207/radical-acceptance.

Hamilton, Patrick. 1939/2005. *Gas Light: A Victorian Thriller.* London: Samuel French.

Hammond, Christine. 2019. "Narcissists and Their Flying Monkeys." *PsychCentral*, July 4, 2019. http://www.psychcentral.com/pro/exhausted-woman/2019/07/narcissists-and-their-flying-monkeys#1.

Holtz, Fred. (2008, revised 2022). *Ten Ways to Stop Anxiety.* Plainview, NY: TherapyMyWay.

Hubbard, Stacy. n.d. "Dating After a Breakup." *The Gottman Institute.* https://www.gottman.com/blog/dating-after-a-breakup.

Hubbard, Stacy. n.d. "How to Heal from Past Relationships." *The Gottman Institute.* http://www.gottman.com/blog/how-to-heal-from-past-relationships.

Kandola, Aaron. 2022. "Signs of Covert Narcissism." *Medical News Today*, May 24, 2022. Updated May 25, 2022. http://www.medicalnewstoday.com/articles/covert-narcissist.

Lamothe, Cindy. 2019. "Got an Overbearing Ex? They Might Be Hoovering." *Healthline*, December 17, 2019. http://www.healthline.com/health/hoovering.

Machiavelli, Niccolò. 1513. *The Prince*. Italy: Public Domain.

MacKenzie, Jackson. 2015. *Psychopath Free: Recovering from Emotionally Abusive Relationships with Narcissists, Sociopaths, and Other Toxic People*. New York: Berkley Books.

Maslow, Abraham. 1954. *Motivation and Personality*. Columbus: Ohio State University Press.

Mayfield, Emily. 2020. "Silent Treatment as a Way to Punish: Stonewalling in Narcissistic Relationships." *Mindset Therapy*, November 18, 2020. http://www.mindsettherapyonline.com/blog/silent-treatment-as-a-way-to-punish-stonewalling-in-narcissistic-relationships.

McBride, Karyl. 2008. *Will I Ever Be Good Enough? Healing the Daughters of Narcissistic Mothers*. New York: Atria, Simon & Schuster.

Mayo Foundation for Medical Education and Research. 2019. "Antisocial Personality Disorder." Mayo Clinic, December 10, 2019. http://www.mayoclinic.org/diseases-conditions/antisocial-personality-disorder/symptoms-causes/syc-20353928.

Morningstar, Dana. 2017. *Out of the Fog: Moving from Confusion to Clarity after Narcissistic Abuse*. Mason, MI: Morningstar Media.

Morris, Kat. 2020. "'False Consensus' Is Why You Vote for Dangerous People." *Medium*, September 27, 2020. https://katmorriswriter.medium.com/false-consensus-is-why-you-vote-for-dangerous-people-52581de7f8ce.

Narcissist Abuse Support. n.d. "Are You Dating a Narcissistic Boyfriend or Girlfriend?" *Narcissist Abuse Support*. https://narcissistabusesupport.com/are-you-dating-a-narcissistic-boyfriend-or-girlfriend.

Ni, Preston. 2012. "7 Keys to Long-Term Relationship Success." *Psychology Today*, October 7, 2012. https://www.psychologytoday.com/us/blog/communication-success/201210/7-keys-long-term-relationship-success.

Ni, Preston. 2019. "7 Ways Narcissists Manipulate Relationships." *Psychology Today*, March 3, 2019. http://www.psychologytoday.com/us/blog/communication-success/201903/7-ways-narcissists-manipulate-relationships.

Nikos-Rose, Karen. 2018. "Long-Term and Short-Term Relationships Initially Indistinguishable." *UC Davis News*, May 14, 2018. https://www.ucdavis.edu/news/long-term-and-short-term-relationships-initially-indistinguishable.

Orwell, George. 1949. *Nineteen Eighty-Four*. New York: Secker and Warburg.

Palmatier, Tara. 2021. "What Do Narcissists Mean By, 'You Can't Survive Without Me?'" *Shrink4Men*, March 5, 2021. https://shrink4men.com/2021/03/05/what-do-narcissists-mean-by-you-cant-survive-without-me/.

Palmatier, Tara, and Paul Elam. 2017. *Say Goodbye to Crazy: How to Get Rid of His Crazy Ex and Restore Sanity to Your Life.* North Charleston, SC: SGCT.

Paulhus, Delroy, and Kevin Williams. 2002. "The Dark Triad of Personality: Narcissism, Machiavellianism, and Psychopathy." *Journal of Research in Personality*, 36(6), 556–563.

Psychology Today Staff. 2021. "Borderline Personality Disorder." *Psychology Today*, August 19, 2021. http://www.psychologytoday.com/us/conditions /borderline-personality-disorder.

Psychology Today Staff. 2022. "Narcissistic Personality Disorder." *Psychology Today*, January 6, 2022. Accessed January 13, 2023, from https://www .psychologytoday.com/us/conditions/narcissistic-personality-disorder.

Raypole, Crystal. 2020. "Echoism: The Other Side of Narcissism." *Healthline*, August 28, 2020. http://www.healthline.com/health/mental-health/echoism.

Romanelli, Assael. 2020. "Flooding: The State That Ruins Relationships." *Psychology Today*, April 28, 2020. http://www.psychologytoday.com/us/blo g/the-other-side-relationships/202004/flooding-the-state-ruins-relationships.

Romano, Lisa A. 2012. *The Road Back to Me: Healing and Recovering from Co-Dependency, Addiction, Enabling, and Low Self-Esteem.* n.p.: Lisa Romano.

Romano, Lisa A. 2020. "The Gaslighting Narcissist." *Lisa A. Romano*, October 19, 2020. https://www.lisaaromano.com/blog/gaslighting-narcissist.

Rosenberg, Ross. 2013. *The Human Magnet Syndrome: Why We Love People Who Hurt Us.* Eau Claire, WI: Premier Publishing & Media.

Spaas, Lieve. 2000. *Echoes of Narcissus.* London: Berghahn Books.

Stevenson, Robert Louis. 1886. *The Strange Case of Dr. Jekyll and Mr. Hyde.* London: Longmans, Green & Co.

Ury, Logan. n.d. "Go for the Life Partner, Not the Prom Date." *The Gottman Institute.* https://www.gottman.com/blog/go-for-the-life-partner-not-the-prom -date.

Vaknin, Sam. 2008. "Narcissists, Narcissistic Supply and Sources of Supply." *HealthyPlace*, November 30, 2008. https://www.healthyplace.com/personality -disorders/malignant-self-love/narcissists-narcissistic-supply-and-sources-of -supply.

Walker, Pete. 2013. *Complex PTSD: From Surviving to Thriving.* Lafayette, CA: Azure Coyote.

Weir, Kirsten. 2018. "Life-Saving Relationships." American Psychological Society, Monitor on Psychology, March 2018. http://www.apa.org/monitor/2018/03 /life-saving-relationships.

Wiesenthal, Simon. 1998. *The Sunflower: On the Possibilities and Limits of Forgiveness.* New York: Schocken Books.

Wilde, Oscar. 1890. *The Picture of Dorian Gray.* New York: Ward, Lock and Co.

ABOUT THE AUTHORS

 **Fred L. Holtz, PhD,** is a licensed clinical psychologist and is executive director of TherapyMyWay, a group practice located in Plainview, New York. His specialties are building social skills, treating panic disorder and phobias, professional practice building, and helping couples through relationship difficulties. For the past ten years, Dr. Holtz has focused on assisting people in recognizing and escaping narcissistic abuse.

Dr. Holtz received his doctorate and master's degree in clinical and school psychology from Hofstra University, his BA in psychology from SUNY Stony Brook, and his AA in liberal arts from Nassau Community College.

His previous publications include *Ten Ways to Stop Anxiety*, a practical booklet on identifying and reducing the symptoms of stress and anxiety. Dr. Holtz has been in private practice for more than thirty-two years and has been a guest lecturer and workshop leader for businesses and nonprofit organizations. His natural and approachable style of therapy, always done with empathy, humor, and sincerity, has helped his clients cope more effectively and reach their personal goals. Dr. Holtz enjoys photography, producing electronic music, graphic design, and gaming. He lives on Long Island, New York, with his wife and young son.

For more information, visit www.TherapyMyWay.com.

. . .

 **Dr. Robin Bryman** is a licensed psychologist. She earned a doctoral degree in school psychology from the City University of New York in 2002 and holds master's degrees in counseling psychology and industrial psychology from Teachers College, Columbia University, earned in 1990. She earned a bachelor's degree in psychology from the State University of New York at Albany in 1988.

Dr. Bryman has had vast experience in the field of psychology over the years. This includes an extensive research background involving children, adolescents, and parenting. She was an adjunct professor at Queens College, teaching both undergraduate and graduate student courses spanning from psychology to elementary and secondary education.

For more than eighteen years, Dr. Bryman has been in private practice specializing in children, adolescents, families, individual counseling, and marital counseling, as well as treating anxiety and depression, and conducting play therapy and parenting training. In addition, she is a specialist in cognitive behavioral therapy and psychodynamic therapy.

More recently, Dr. Bryman has become an expert in narcissist abuse recovery. In her private practice, she treats individuals and runs a group. By sharing recovery strategies from both a clinical and a personal perspective, Dr. Bryman helps clients recover from all aspects of this complex type of abuse. Issues range from the inability to break free completely from a relationship to struggles with C-PTSD and self-blame.

Dr. Bryman's narcissist abuse recovery group meets twice a month. A consultation and assignments are required for entry into the group. For more information or to schedule an appointment, please visit Dr. Robin Bryman via Psychology Today (psychologytoday.com) and/or her website at www.drrobinbryman.com.

WHAT IS THE BEST WAY TO CONTACT THE AUTHORS?

Websites: www.ByeByeNarcissist.com,
www.TherapyMyWay.com

Twitter: ByeByeNarcissist @ByeByeNarc

Facebook: @ByeByeNarcissist

Instagram: ByeByeNarcissist

TikTok: ByeNarcissist, TherapyMyWay

FRED L. HOLTZ, PHD

Fred@ByeByeNarcissist.com
(for issues related to narcissists)

Fred@TherapyMyWay.com
(for psychological issues in general)

(516) 888-HELP

DR. ROBIN BRYMAN:

DrRobinBryman@gmail.com

www.drrobinbryman.com

JILLIAN LEE (ILLUSTRATOR)

markertherapy@gmail.com

www.markertherapy.com